From Saint to Shark
The Cliff Watson Story

From Saint to Shark

The Cliff Watson Story

Cliff Watson with Tom Mather

Vertical Editions
www.verticaleditions.com

First published in the United Kingdom in 2017 by Vertical Editions, Unit 4a, Snaygill Industrial Estate, Skipton, North Yorkshire BD23 2QR

Originally published as an ebook by Tom Mather in 2015

www.verticaleditions.com

ISBN 978-1-904091-99-8

A CIP catalogue record for this book is available from the British Library

Cover design by HBA, York

Printed and bound by CMP (uk) Ltd, Poole, Dorset

Contents

This book is dedicated to my wife, Barbara, and my daughters, Gaynor, Tina and Kareena, who have supported me every step of the way.

Cliff Watson

Acknowledgements

In a book such as this it is easy to think that all that is needed is the input from the player. While that may be true, the richness of the book increases greatly for the reader if contributions are included from others who were involved with the story. In this respect I would like to thank all of those players who felt so positively about Cliff that they willingly added their own recollections of him.

My heartfelt thanks go to Ray French, not only for his own reminisences of Cliff, but also for kindly agreeing to write the foreword to the book. Also to Billy Benyon, Alex Murphy, John Mantle, Tommy Bishop and John Warlow from the St. Helens club for their contributions. And to Ronnie Turner, Bobby Wear, Ken Maddison, Greg Pierce and John Dorahy for their memories of Cliff's time down in Sydney.

My appreciation goes to Bernard Platt for the photograph of the St. Helens Greatest 17 Players, and to the Saints Heritage Society for many of the superb images of Cliff in his playing days at St. Helens. Other photographs are taken from Cliff's own scrapbooks, and to those who may have taken them and given them to him as memento, I am indebted to you for your consideration and your efforts.

Finally thanks must go to Mike Critchley for pointing

the way to getting this book published, and to all those who touched on Cliff's playing career. From team-mates and opponents to coaches, fans, administrators and pressmen, you helped make this book what it is – a record of Cliff Watson's Rugby League life and of the game as it was played in the 'good old days'.

Tom Mather

Foreword

To reply to a newspaper advert urging young Rugby Union players to try their hand at the rival code of Rugby League certainly takes confidence on the part of anyone attempting to master the 13-a-side game. It takes real courage when that player, with little knowledge of the game, is attempting to move from a then minor Rugby Union club in the Midlands of England, to one of the most celebrated professional clubs in the history of the breakaway code – St. Helens. Especially when he is seeking to force his way into a pack of forwards, all of whom were internationals and containing three British Lions tourists of the calibre of Dick Huddart, Abe Terry, and the legendary Vince Karalius. Confidence, courage, and ambition indeed on Cliff's part!

Such characteristics were at the heart of the powerful England prop forward's drive to the top in Rugby League. As a newcomer myself from the world of Rugby Union, and a member of that same St. Helens pack just six months after Cliff's own arrival at Knowsley Road, he proved a staunch ally on and off the field. His commitment, ambition and confidence set the standards for myself. His courage was never in doubt, setting the example for all whenever the hard yards needed to be made close to our own try line, and always being on hand whenever any were tiring in the demanding final quarter of a particularly hard match – no substitutes or interchange benches in operation in days of yore.

His sense of humour and spirit in the dressing room enabled many to rise to the occasion, and never was he more valuable to a team and myself than when I had the pleasure of playing alongside him on the World Cup British Lions Tour of Australia and New Zealand in 1968. Whatever difficulties he faced on and off the pitch, he conquered them with the same determination that made him one of the finest of prop forwards to play the game both in the British Isles and in Australasia. But particularly Cliff should be acknowledged for the fine friend and support he was to all who came into contact with him, and especially to me during the early days of my own conversion to a new code.

Cliff Watson's rugby career scaled the heights and was filled with drama, tension, glory, and occasionally despair on the field. It was filled with fun, humour, friendship and camaraderie among his team-mates off the pitch. His account of that career makes for what I am sure will be a wonderful read for any rugby follower of either code.

Ray French

Introduction

Saturday May 13th, 1961 was, and still is in the eyes of many older supporters, the biggest day in the calendar of that Rugby League season. It was the day of the Challenge Cup Final played at Wembley Stadium. It was a game that drew tens of thousands of fans down to London, whichever Rugby League team they supported. That afternoon was no different but it did have the added spice of being a derby final, a final between two of the oldest and fiercest rivals in the game in Wigan and St. Helens. Any game between these two teams has always been keenly contested, but the ante had been racked up even further as this was Wembley and a Challenge Cup Final.

The afternoon was scorching hot and sapped the energy of the players of both clubs, even the fans sitting in shirt sleeves, almost 95,000 of them, were wilting in the heat just watching the action. As the players went into the dressing room at half time, it was the white shirt with the red vee of the St. Helens team that held the advantage, but only by the narrow margin of 5-2. The great Alex Murphy had crossed for a try and Austin Rhodes had added two more points, while all the red shirted Wigan team had to show was a goal from South African full back Fred 'Punchy' Griffiths.

As the players re-entered the field for the second

half, it was only then that it finally dawned on one young Saints forward just what he was involved in. As Cliff Watson walked out onto the pitch for the start of the final 40 minutes, he saw a mass of red and white that looked like a huge, high wall surrounding the pitch, that wall was making a sound unlike anything he had ever experienced. It made walking out onto the pitch seem like he was walking through treacle.

As the second half got under way, the action followed that of the first. Defences were to the fore and the game moved from end to end – it was one of those games that could have gone either way. Then for the first time, a little bit of magic from the Wigan team saw the wingman, Billy Boston, break away and head for the Saints try line. The whole stadium rose to their feet and roared, the Wigan fans with expectation, the Saints fans in desperation. Everyone knew that in such situations it was odds-on that the blockbusting Boston would score he was, generally speaking, unstoppable once in his stride in such situations.

In any game of Rugby League when the score is close, both teams are evenly matched and there is a lot at stake, there will come a time when one piece of action will alter the whole course of the game, the so-called game-breaking play. In most cases such plays involve a piece of individual brilliance from an attacking player to score a match-winning try, a drop goal to take the lead, or a memorable penalty goal, but not always; sometimes it is the defender that pulls out something really special.

As Boston headed down the wing for the try line, one player was seen haring across the pitch in an attempt to make a cover tackle on him. That player was Cliff Watson the young Saints prop. It was something that prop forwards in that era usually never did, but then Watson was not your usual prop forward. Incredibly Watson came thundering across the pitch, closing in on the Wigan wingman, and eventually pulled off a tackle on Boston that all the pundits would later agree changed the course of the Final. Watson lined up Boston, got his angles right and surprised everyone with the speed at which he covered the ground. The result was a copybook cover tackle that crashed Boston to the ground over the touchline and saved a try.

Had Boston scored in the corner as was expected, then Wigan were back in the game, and the momentum generated could have seen them go on and take the spoils. As it was, Watson's wonder tackle spurred the Saints players on to even greater efforts, and late in the game they clinched the win with one of the best tries ever seen at the old stadium when Tom van Vollenhoven and Ken Large conjured up a length-of-the-field piece of action, ending with 'Tommy Voll' touching down behind the posts. That match-winning try epitomised the Final and has become etched into supporters' minds. Consequently people have often forgotten the magnificent game-saving tackle made earlier by Watson.

When the dust settled and wise people in the game had had time to analyse the action, they realised the importance of Watson's effort in tackling Boston and also questioned how a prop forward could cover across the field like a loose forward or a wingman. This was not something that was in the average prop forward's locker. The young prop had, with that single tackle, as they say 'arrived' but his arrival into the game in general, just like his arrival at that final and acceptance by the fans, was equally as strange and thought provoking.

Watson was not your normal jobbing prop approaching his 30s who had served his apprenticeship in the A-team for five years or more, learning the dark arts of the front row of the scrum. Watson was a 21-year-old, playing only his 11th game of Rugby League, having joined St. Helens in the most peculiar of circumstances. He was a one-off and he was to go on to forge a career that put him at the forefront of the game on two continents. He was a forward out of the very top drawer who would go on to achieve legendary status. He became a prop noted for never taking a backward step and, even more importantly for the British fans, being able to dominate the game in the international arena.

However, it all started so very differently for the young Cliff Watson in 1961, when he was just making his way in the game …

Tom Mather

1

Early Days

I was born in April 1940 when the horrors of the Second World War were really hitting home, particularly in London. I suppose it could be said that I was born a Cockney, having seen the light of day for the first time in Stepney in North London. It was not a hot bed of rugby for either code, it was football and the Arsenal that generated the sporting passions of people in that part of the world. In truth, if Adolph Hitler had not had grand designs to take over the British Isles, then I probably would not have had a career as a Rugby League player. Mum and dad had five children – myself and two brothers and two sisters and, while we lived in London, dad was actually born in Dudley in the Midlands.

Early in the war when the blitz was at its height, we actually got bombed out by the Luftwaffe. When it happened, mum and dad took us all back into the Dudley area, moving in with an aunt and uncle. When the war came to an end they never went back to the capital, so it was in Dudley that I grew up.

As a kid growing up I was like everyone else in the area, no one had much money and it was a case of making your own entertainment. We played the usual games of football and cricket in the street as there were very few cars around. It was only when I went to school that I experienced sport that was organised.

When I was 15 the local Rugby Union club, Dudley Kingswinford, approached the school to see if anyone wanted to play for them. I had played little organised sport as a kid simply because I had suffered from chronic ingrown toenails, particularly on my big toes. Nothing seemed to cure the problem and it stopped my playing games as a youngster. In the end it was decided that the nails on my two big toes would be removed along with the roots. Once I recovered I was better able to play sports, although I was no good at soccer being so big and having no toenails.

At school I was better at athletics than anything else but I decided I would give rugby a go. We only played about four games before the whole thing folded, but it was funny in the beginning. As the guys from the club lined all the kids up who wanted to take part, they said things like, 'You look like you can run fast so you can play on the wing, you're very tall you're going to play second-row,' and so on. At the end of the process everyone except me had been given a position to play so I said, 'What about me?' The reply came back, 'You're the hooker'. I thought, 'That will do for me,' so I played at hooker in those four games and they were to give me a love for rugby that I was never to lose.

When I was 16 and had left school, the club set up a colts side and I went down there and started to play regularly as a hooker. Eventually I got in the first team but by then I had grown so played as a second-row forward rather than at hooker. Back then I was around 15 and a half stone and I was reasonably quick – particularly for the standard and position I was playing.

Dudley Kingswinford were very much a junior club. If we had a fixture against a club such as Coventry, who were one of the big clubs in the Midlands, then we would find ourselves playing against their third team or the likes. But despite this I started to make a name for myself in junior rugby club circles around Dudley, although I was surprised when I was asked to play in a trial for the Worcester and Hereford combined counties side. It was not something that happened to players at junior clubs, Rugby Union was very elitist then and probably still is.

I was asked to play at prop in the trial, rather than second-row, as I was not tall enough. At county level, the second-rows were often six feet, six inches and taller, while I was just about six feet, so at prop I played. In truth I was an ideal build for a prop, and being strong I was able to scrummage very well.

I was very pleased when I got selected for the county but it was really an eye-opener. I thought I was doing well for myself driving an old Ford Popular, but others in the team were driving around in Jaguars and such like. County level rugby was a different world and I remember on one occasion when I was approached by one of the committee members after a training session and asked what I wanted with regards to my expenses. I had no idea what to ask for but said to the guy just give me five shillings for my petrol. He looked down his nose at me and replied, 'My dear boy, nowhere near enough, here take a pound!'

I was proud to be selected for the combined counties side and I think I was the first player from the club to get county honours. I am not sure if anyone from Dudley Kingswinford has been selected for the county since.

In 1960 I was just 20 years old and working as a toolmaker at Newey Brothers at Tipton. The company made press studs, zips, bra fasteners and suchlike. I had played in a Rugby Union seven-a-side competition for the club at the end of the season and suffered a scaphoid fracture in my wrist. My boss at work was a good chap and let me come into the factory and work in the stores as I could not do my own job as an apprentice tool-maker due to the injury. Back then if you were off work you didn't get any pay, so I was glad to be in the stores and still earning a wage. One morning the guy I was working with in the stores came over and said to me, 'Hey Cliff what sort of money do Rugby League players get paid?' I had no idea but asked him why and it was then he showed me the advert that the St. Helens secretary, Basil Lowe, had placed in the *Sporting Chronicle*. It said that St. Helens were looking for top class Rugby Union forwards to trial with the club.

He actually cut the advert out of the paper and gave it to me, and luckily I stuffed it in my pocket to have a good look at later. When I read it carefully I thought, well I know bugger-all about Rugby League or what the pay is but I have been selected for the combined counties so maybe that makes me a top quality Rugby Union forward. The one thing I was sure of was that I should not say a word about my plans to anyone. Back then even talking to a professional club was enough to get you into serious trouble with the Rugby Football Union, but I decided I might as well have a go. If the St. Helens club didn't want me then all it would cost me would be the price of a stamp and then I'd carry on playing Rugby Union.

That night when I got home my girlfriend, Barbara (later my wife), sat down with me and we talked about what I should do. Eventually we composed a letter to the Saints club, which Barbara wrote for me as my arm was still in plaster. I briefly told them who I was and what I had achieved in my career to that time. The advert said, 'Are you over six feet?', which I wasn't, so I asked Barbara to put in the letter that I was six feet and three quarters, which she did. Then we posted off the letter and settled back to wait and see what happened.

When I got the invitation to go up and train with the club I had only had the plaster off my wrist for two weeks but I didn't tell anyone. Fortunately the first trial game I should have played for Saints was rained off and so I got an extra week to improve my fitness and to let the wrist heal and strengthen.

As I drove up to the ground for the first training session, I wondered what the club was expecting, as the way we had written the letter it could have been thought that I was actually six feet, nine inches tall and 15 and a half stone! Thankfully no one questioned my height and weight at the club.

When I arrived at St. Helens, the club already had a number of former Rugby Union players in the squad so I was instantly made welcome and quickly accepted by the lads I was training with. When I started regularly travelling up to St. Helens to train and play, Barbara and I decided to work out what I should ask for if they wanted to sign me. At the time we were looking to get married and buy a house in Dudley – a Joseph Webb-built semi-detached which we thought was very posh. We agreed we would be happy if I got £200 but I was going to try hard to get a bit more if I could. That sort of money would have put the pair of us well on the way to being able to buy the house.

I played my first trial game at Knowsley Road against

Liverpool but it was difficult to know just how well I had performed. I had played in county trials in Rugby Union where each player had a specific job to do. That was not the case in League, so I just went out and put myself about. I reckoned if I worked hard and caught the eye of the directors then I would do okay. I had a chuckle when I saw the match programme, as everything had to be done in secret, but the club programme writer had a sense of humour as he put me in the programme as A.N. Martha. I remember that Liverpool had a prop playing against me named Brian Cox. He bullied me all the game and kept head-butting me when we scrummed down and his forehead was like it had been hewn from solid oak!

After the match I was sat in the big bath in the dressing room with the rest of the lads when Basil Lowe came in. He called me over and asked for a quiet word.

'Well Cliff, we like your style of play and we are pleased with your performance today, we would like to sign you. The only question now is just how much you are looking for?' Basil said.

Even to this day I cannot for the life of me work out how I had the gall to say what I said. All the conversations I'd had with Barbara went to the back of my mind as I looked Basil straight in the eye and quick as a flash said, 'I'm looking for £2,000'.

Basil replied, 'No way,' and went on to say that the board had decided they would give international players £2000 but would only give £1,500 to non-international players.

I tried my best to keep calm, swallowed hard and said, 'Okay, if that is the best you can do I'll accept £1,500.

I then got dressed and Basil took me up to the

boardroom and placed a contract in front of me. To tell the truth I was so excited I couldn't focus on reading the bloody thing but I scanned through it and said it looked fine and I signed the contract there and then.

I drove back to the Midlands as quick as I could and Barbara asked how I had gone on in the match and if they wanted to sign me. I told her they did so she asked if I'd managed to get more than the £200 we had talked about. She could not believe it when I told her the figure was £1,500!

When we got down to the negotiations and the fine detail, it was agreed that I would get £750 to sign for the club and another £750 when I played six first team games. The first £750 was tax free but the second payment I had to pay tax on. But the thing was that back then, when you signed for a club, you signed for life, unlike today when you sign a contract for a specific period of time. When I had arrived at the club, I remember Harry Cook, one of the directors, telling me after training one night that I would probably be playing in the reserves for about five or six years in order to learn the game. I thought shit, I am 20 now, I do not want to be waiting that long to make it in this game. However, after a few weeks I was selected to play for the first team against Liverpool City.

When I played that first game in the first team, I really did not know what I was doing. I went out there as a snotty-nosed kid and kept on running the ball up and putting myself about, trying to tackle anyone and everyone. I thought that was what I needed to do to impress but I remember Vince Karalius telling the coach, Alan Prescott, that I was interfering with the plays they were running and making a bloody nuisance of myself. Vince told the coach to get me out of the way so the forwards could play their game without interference. He told Prescott to put me out on the wing where I could not do any damage. That was where I finished up and I can remember vividly running at the wingman, a bloke named Bright – me a front row forward and him a bloody wingman. We lost the game but I must have done enough for the club to see that I had potential.

> *Cliff came to Saints from Rugby Union and, in my opinion, he became one of St. Helens' best ever signings. He learned quickly as he went along once he got into the first team. Cliff was a big, strong bloke and I remember him working as a drayman for the brewery. He could lift up a full barrel of beer back then, so tackling a player was no problem for him.*
>
> *People still talk about his tackle on Billy Boston at Wembley and I believe that 99 times out of a hundred Billy would have scored that try; it was a fantastic tackle. There was not another prop playing then who would have been fast enough to cover across and get to Billy, let alone tackle him. He was never the best handler of a ball but, once he got hold of it and charged forward, you needed a stick of dynamite to get it out of his grasp. Cliff was one of those players you loved to play with and hated to play against. I have always liked winners and Cliff was a winner. Off the field he was a lovely fellow who fitted in well with the Saints team which, back then, was like one big family.*

Alex Murphy

I must say in those early days at the club that I owed a great deal to the Saints coach, Alan Prescott, who spent a good deal of time with me. Coming from Rugby Union, my handling of the ball was not good. Mind you it never was – I was never a ball-playing prop in the mould of a Brian McTigue at Wigan. Alan had me throwing the ball against a wall and catching the rebound in an effort to improve my handling. I would do that after training for half an hour just to quicken up my reflexes. The other advantage I had was that there were a lot of experienced players in the side that were able to guide me. Players like Vince Karalius, Dick Huddart, Don Vines, Abe Terry and Bob Dagnall who were all internationals.

Back then the scrums were real scrums and we played unlimited tackles, so if you lost the ball you would often be playing defensively for 10 minutes or more until you regained possession. I learned a great deal from Dagnall about playing blind side prop. My job was not really to push in the scrum, as it was in Rugby Union, but to try to pull my opposite prop down and hold the opposition pack while I did so. Daggy was always calling out to me to 'Pull him down Cliff.' I must have learned quickly because I eventually played 11 times in the first team that first season and the 11th game was actually at Wembley!

The whole of that first season as a professional was a culture shock for me in every way. I had no idea of the history of the game, the relationships that existed and the rivalry between the different clubs. It was something I had never experienced playing Union in the Midlands. The Rugby Union I played was really a social affair, unlike professional Rugby League. Win or lose, you still had a good time when I was at Dudley, but it was a lot different at St. Helens.

It was sometime around April 1961 that I really got an extended run with the first team and I found myself going over to Odsal Stadium to play against Hull in the semifinal of the Challenge Cup. It was a bit of a shock for me getting selected, but an even bigger one for the press boys who had a field day. They are always looking for an angle or a headline and I gave them one when the club announced the semifinal line-up. They made a big thing of the fact that I had been selected over Fred Leyland and Jim Measures, who were both more experienced than me, and pointed out that I would be playing against the very experienced Jim Drake in the Hull front row. I hadn't a clue who Jim Drake was, he could well have been Charlie Drake for all I knew about him. I just took the view that the coach had picked me to play so he must have thought I could do the job for the team. To be fair, I was not particularly interested in whether Measures or Leyland should have been playing or what they thought, I was just chuffed that Prescott had picked me for such an important game.

My aim in the semi was to play well and try and cement my place in the pack, so that hopefully I'd make the line-up if we got to the Final. I made my mind up as I sat in the dressing room waiting for the game to start that nothing would get past me that day, and I bet I was not far off making a couple of hundred tackles during the game. At the end we walked off the field winning by 26-9. Hull just never had a chance that afternoon as we tackled them out of the game and starved them of the ball with Daggy winning the scrums. I was amazed at the reaction of some of some of my team-mates over the win and getting to the Final at Wembley. To me it was just another game and I could not understand what all the bloody fuss was about but I was soon to find out!

We did not have the best of preparations for the Wembley Final as the Saturday before we played Leeds in the semifinal of the Championship – the top four play-off as it was called back then. We did not really perform as we should have and lost the game 11-4. Of course, everyone said it was because we had our mind on the Wembley game, which again was something I could not understand. The reasoning that we had missed getting to the Championship Final because our minds were on playing in another cup final the following week made no sense to me.

If truth be told we should not really have even got into the top four play-off that season. We had dropped out of the top four just before the semifinal against Hull and were due to play up at Hull in the league a few weeks before the cup game. So, because the board thought we were out of contention for the Championship, they sent what was virtually an A-team to the Boulevard. I was in the line-up with many of the other A-team players alongside a few experienced heads, including Abe Terry and Fred Leyland. Whereas Hull played a full strength side which included most of their semifinal line-up. But bugger me, we turned them over that day and climbed back into the top four as a result. I tackled my heart out in that game, and when I tackled a player I stayed as marker and stepped whichever way the ball went then put in the next tackle – and the next. It must have been an impressive showing from us because the reporter for the St. Helens newspaper wrote of that game:

> Watson, Donegan, Fred Terry, Finney ... on paper just ordinary A-team players, rarely capable of challenging for a first team place against opposition like Huddart, Vince Karalius and Murphy. But on the bare expanse of The Boulevard they turned out the finest displays of their young careers – their fighting spirit succeeded where that of regulars had failed and shot the fallen star that was Saints back into the top four fight.

I remember that Tommy Voll had written an article for the local paper just prior to the Hull semifinal and got a lot of stick for saying the club was justified in doing what it had done in sending the A-team up to Hull. After all, as he said, the A-team had won and all the first team players were fit and healthy for the semifinal. But as we walked out of the dressing room and down all those steps through the crowd at Odsal, the Hull supporters did not see it like that and really gave it to Tommy in particular and the rest of us too. I can tell you it was a bloody long way down from that old dressing room to the pitch at Odsal.

After the loss to Leeds in the Championship I was a bit worried but I managed to keep my place in the team for Wembley. The club took us away and put us into camp at Ilkley Moor. It was the same place that the Aussies used when they came over on tour. We trained up there, and then a couple of days before the game we moved down to London. I had to get time off work but that did not seem to be a problem as all the local firms seemed to be supporters of the club.

I couldn't understand what all the fuss and bother was about. Why did we need to go into camp just to play a cup final and why were we all given a 'Wembley suit' to wear on the day? I should have realised then that this game was something special but I still thought it was a lot of fuss about nothing. The problem was that as we were away in Yorkshire, we did not see the St. Helens paper or any of the hype in the local area so I did not experience any of the build up to the game.

In truth it could have all been so very different and who knows if my career would have taken the path it eventually did. I was not really involved in the Challenge

Cup until we got to the semifinal and our cup run, in that first season for me at the club, could have been all over before it had begun. In the first round we had drawn Widnes at home who were close and fierce rivals. Widnes were not the cup kings they were to become but, whenever they played Saints, they needed a government health warning on their shirts such was the ferocity with which they played. We only just managed to scramble a draw 5-5 and lucky for us they could not raise their game in the replay as we won through 29-10. In the next round the club travelled over to Castleford, which was never an easy trip, but we won 18-10 and then we beat Swinton at home 17-9.

I often think what would have happened had Widnes won that first round tie. There would have been no Wembley appearance for me, no well-remembered tackle and performance that afternoon and perhaps I may well have, as Harry Cook said, spent the next five or six years learning my trade in the A-team. I may well never have become a regular first team player at the club! It is on such little things a player's career can turn.

On the day of the Final again it really did not hit me just how big an occasion this game was. We arrived early at the ground and walked onto the pitch as fans were beginning to come into the stadium. When I went down the tunnel to the dressing rooms, I couldn't hear the crowd and had no idea just how big it was to grow to. The dressing rooms were so far away from the pitch that the crowd singing and cheering just did not reach us.

I don't remember too much about the game as I think I was too young and inexperienced for it to sink in. I do recall being lined up and introduced to the crowd but the first half seemed to pass by in no time. I remember Alex Murphy scored a try to give us the lead. However, Murphy was a natural talent and so quick thinking that it wasn't surprising when he scored.

In the dressing room at half time Prescott was pleased, not just because we were leading but also because we had not had our line crossed. The score was 5-2 and our defence had been good. Mind you, we could have actually gone in 6-5 down had Wigan converted two penalties that they really should have put over. In the dressing room Prescott had us all drinking water with salt in due to the fact that it was a blistering hot afternoon; he wanted us to replace the salt we had lost sweating during that first 40 minutes.

It was only when we walked out for the second half that I realised just what I was involved in. As I walked out of the darkness of the tunnel and into the bright sunshine, I could not believe what I saw. We played in red and white and Wigan in cherry and white and all I could see was a wall of red and white that went right round the stadium. Then the roar hit me and the noise the crowd made was unbelievable. I remember as I walked out and looked around thinking, 'Bloody hell, this is it, I have made it!'

When the second half got going, it seemed to follow the same pattern as the first, with both defences on top. Then Wigan swung the ball out to the wing and Billy Boston set off down the touchline. As I had played a lot of second-row in Union, I was used to covering across the field in defence. It was not something that props did in the game back then, but in those early days I was around 15 and a half stone when usually the props were much bigger and slower. I set off covering across the pitch and tried to cut down the angle so I could reach Boston before he got to the try line. At the time I had no idea just who Billy Boston was, he could just as well have been Billy Bunter for all I knew. Luckily I got across and made the tackle – I hit him right in the thigh and knocked him over the touchline and saved the try. I thought nothing of it at the time and got on with the game. It was only afterwards when the game was over that people began to say that the tackle was a game-saver. To me it was just another tackle, something I had done my entire Rugby Union career.

We went on to win the game and Tommy Voll scored one of the best tries ever seen at the old Wembley, scorching over the line from the wing. I remember walking up those steps at the end of the game to get my winner's medal and turning round to see the mass of fans cheering their heads off. I realised then it was a very special occasion. I was just 21 years old, my birthday was the 26th of April and the game was on the 13th of May. I had progressed from junior Rugby Union to Challenge Cup winner in around nine months. I remember after the game there were quite a number of people who felt that I should have won the Lance Todd Trophy.

I had defended well all the game, it was not just the tackle on Boston that pleased me, I had also caught and tackled the scrum-half, Terry Entwistle, which had surprised everyone. In addition I'd done a fair bit of work taking the ball up and supporting when a break was made. I remember late in the game Dick Huddart made a break and he could shift a bit, but I went up and supported him and took the pass to drive even deeper into the Wigan half of the pitch.

Some of the press boys told me after the game that

the only reason I had not got the vote as man of the match was because I was an unknown newcomer. The reporter from the *Daily Mirror* got a bit upset that I had not won the Lance Todd Trophy. I think he had actually voted for me and he made a big thing about me being the first Cockney to play in a Rugby League Final at Wembley. Instead they presented me with the 'Andy Capp Trophy'. It was a hound's tooth check Andy Capp style cap and inside it said: 'The Andy Capp. Presented to Cliff Watson. With best wishes from the *Daily Mirror*.'

To my knowledge it is the only such cap in existence and something I still treasure to this day. I still have the poster from outside the local news agents that read in big letters: AN ANDY CAPP FOR CLIFF WATSON

Pilkington Glass, who were based in the town, got all of the players from that winning side together and collected their signatures. They then manufactured a limited edition drinking glass on to which all our autographs were incorporated and presented one to each player. That is also something I still treasure.

The other thing I got from winning the cup was an appearance, with the rest of the team, on the Ken Dodd Show. Having won through to Wembley we were invited to the show and spent a day in the studio rehearsing and recording. I remember there was an Aussie juggler who was quite popular at the time. As well as juggling he had this droll patter which was quite funny. He would complain about having to juggle and would throw a ball away which would bounce straight back to him. The finale to his act involved him balancing a golf ball on the end of a thin stick while juggling. In rehearsals Dick Huddart was looking at his equipment and noticed that the golf ball had a little tiny hole drilled in it and the stick had a pin sticking out of it so the golf ball could not fall off! Just as the guy was about to go on stage in front of the audience to do his act, Huddart quietly said to him, 'Marra you will be okay, I have just swopped the golf ball for one of mine.' The juggler nearly crapped himself but had to go out there. We were all cracking up when Dick told us what he had said.

> *I had only just signed for Saints when Cliff arrived at the Knowsley Road. I remember the club had advertised for big forwards to come and trial and Cliff made a big impact right from the beginning. I went down to watch the 1961 Final with the other lads in the A-team and Cliff had a terrific game. He was a big man but he had what no other prop in our game at that time had which was great pace; he really got around the pitch and was also running at opponents out wide, which props did not do then. I don't think there was another front row forward in the game at that time capable of doing what Cliff could do. He looked after me when I started to break into the first team and when I was established. When I went down to Australia he was a great help and support to me and my family. Cliff was supposedly never a drinker as a player, but every Sunday morning, he and his mate would call round at my house and have a glass of milk – with a couple of tots of whisky in it just to give it a bit of body.*

> *Billy Benyon St. Helens*

When the dust had settled after the Final and I was able to take stock of what had happened to me in a little under a year, I was very pleased with the decision I'd made to turn professional. I had just completed my first season in the game and got a Challenge Cup winner's medal – something most players strived for and many went through their whole career and never got. I had

31

just missed out on playing in the Championship Final and was playing for one of the top clubs in the league. I was a very happy man but little did I know just what other honours were waiting ahead for me. One thing I was very proud of was that, following that Wembley Final, I never played reserve grade Rugby League again!

2

A Saint

When I signed for St. Helens, they were insistent on me moving up from the Midlands to the town. Barbara and I had to change our plans. The house we had our eye on down in Dudley was ditched and we decided to quickly get married before we moved up to St. Helens. Back then it was not the done thing to live together if you were not married. The news of my signing as a professional was not universally welcomed back in Dudley. I still have a cutting from the local paper where the reporter – an ex player – wrote of my move:

> I have seen Cliff Watson twice and I wish him the best of luck in his new sphere. He will find rugger, even in St. Helens 'A' XIII, a different proposition from the class he has been playing down this way.

I do remember I went back to my old Rugby Union club on one occasion and got a load of abuse from one member of the club over my switching codes. I quietly reminded him that I had my wife in the car and did not take kindly to him swearing at me. I think it was something like that, but it may well have been a little more colourful and threatening because he quickly cleared off and left me and Barbara alone. That was what it was like back then, players who turned professional were ostracised by the Rugby Union fraternity

Once we settled in the North West, I found that the money I was getting from playing the game was allowing me and Barbara to live reasonably well, so I did not need to get a job. The club were unhappy with that and said that I really needed to be working in the area, and so I had to look around for a job. I found out later that their attitude was a throwback to the very early days of the game, whereby if a player was not working then they could not play for their club. The problem was that a lot of local firms did not really like hiring professional Rugby League players, simply because they had to ask for a great deal of time off work.

The club, through its contacts, got me an interview at a local coal mine and when I turned up they gave me a medical which I easily passed. During the later interview I told them I was a fitter and would be happy working as such above ground. As the interview came to an end they said I had the job and could start on Monday so I asked them about tools. They replied that I would not need them as I would be working at the coal face so I told them to bugger off and left. There was no way I was ever going to work underground. Eventually I got a job working with Alan Prescott and then I went to work as a labourer for Harry Pilling who was a bricklayer.

I did not really suffer the so-called second season dip in form. I think that was because I was still relatively unknown. Having not played a lot of first grade games in my first season, many opposition players didn't know how to deal with me. Also I was still learning the game and improving all the time. Bob Dagnall wanted me to pull my opposite number down as low as possible in the scrums while holding the opposition pack off him. He used to moan at me if he thought I wasn't doing it right so one day I threatened to deck him if he didn't stop complaining – but I never did!

In that second season I was playing against props I had never faced before and I used to try and learn from them. Every prop had a different technique or different tricks they used once they packed down. I learned from them the little things that went on in the scrum that the referee did not see. I think also I was quite quick for a prop and perhaps played a different style of game than props normally did. The huge props around at that time did not move as quickly, so in open play I was able to use my speed either when tackling or trying not to get tackled.

I quickly learned that I had to look after myself at all times on the field. They say to boxers at the start of a fight to defend themselves at all times and I had to do the same. There were some hard men playing the game back then. Frank Foster was a case in point and I am sure that bugger used to sharpen his elbows before he went out onto the field. He was always leading with them, either when he was tackling or running at you with the ball. You could be sure that if you went in and tackled him high you would get an elbow in your throat or chest. You could almost guarantee at some point in the game Frank would get you with an elbow. At Wigan they had Frank Collier and John Barton. They were big, big men and when they hit you, you felt it. John Barton was not a dirty player at all – he had no need to be, he was just so big that when he hit you in the tackle your bloody head started spinning. Frank Collier was a nice guy off the pitch but when he tackled you in a game, you stayed tackled.

Other hard men in the game at the time included

Charlie Winslade at Warrington, who was at the back end of his career but still a handful, and there was Derek 'Rocky' Turner at Wakefield Trinity. Both were great players but very tough.

Our own hard man was Vince Karalius who even scared the crap out of me at times. He would go into his hate mode before a game when he set about building up the dislike he had for this player or that player in the team we were playing that day. On one occasion I went into the dressing room and just shouted, 'Hi Vince how is it going?' He let out a huge roar and the veins on his forehead stood out, so I quickly moved out of his way. That was his way of psyching himself up for a game. Vince and Rocky Turner never did see eye to eye and it used to make for a big showdown whenever they faced each other. Vince also disliked Don Vines with a passion. The club had done a swap with Wakefield with one of our lads going to them and Don coming over the hill to us. I will say a little more about Vince and Don later.

One guy that was a hard nut but also a character was Len McIntyre, the Oldham hooker as he was then. I remember one game when we travelled up to Watersheddings and we did not have a hooker. I told the coach that I would have a go as I had played hooker in Rugby Union. When we lined up for the first scrum, Len looked at our front row and his eyes were like saucers as he said, 'How the bloody hell am I supposed to hook the ball against those three buggers, look at the bloody size of them?' He didn't, I think we won the scrums three to one that afternoon.

But the daddy of the hard men without doubt, either in England or down in Australia, was Brian McTigue who was in a league of his own. Brian was a lovely lad but you never wanted to get on the wrong side of him. We played Wigan at Knowsley Road one Saturday afternoon and I had been putting myself about and must have upset him. I took the ball, lined Brian up and ran straight at him. Brian hit me with a short right hand as he tackled me and I spent the next 70 minutes wandering around the pitch in a daze.

McTigue was the only player I reckon who could hit and really hurt me. He was the silent assassin as no one ever saw him hit you, certainly not the referee; but more importantly the player being hit never saw the punch coming either! I never saw him swing a punch in a game and I was up close to the action. His punch must have travelled no more than four or five inches but you knew when it landed – or more accurately when you came round! The thing with Brian was, as an ex-boxer he had learned to control his anger and you never saw him lose his temper on the field. He just controlled his emotions, threw one short punch and that was it. He was also a wonderful ball player which made him a bloody tough opponent to play against!

The one player who I had a constant problem with was the Leigh prop, Stan Owen. He really was a nasty piece of work and he and I never saw eye to eye throughout my career. In one game I came in to make a tackle on him, and as I was about to grab him I slipped. The result was that instead of tackling him round the waist I grabbed him by the 'nuts'. It was a pure accident as it was always an unwritten rule that you never go for a player in that area. I reckon Owen thought I had done it deliberately as he never forgave or forgot. In another game he was the one doing the tackle and he hit me square in the eye with his elbow. There was no doubt in my mind he did so deliberately but you would have difficulty proving it. At the time it was quite a serious injury and, as the directors were taking me to the hospital, there was a real fear that I may lose the sight in that eye. They were furious, wanting to take legal action against Owen. I told them that they could not do so as it could be near enough impossible to prove that Owen had deliberately hit me. Yes you had to be wary around the Leigh prop.

The list of hard men was endless. Mick Scott and Johnny Whiteley up at Hull along with the Drake twins were not to be messed with. Then on the other end of the scale was the likes of Harold Poynton over at Wakefield. He would chip the ball over the top and then run into the nearest player and go down like a dying swan, and it worked every time as the referee always gave him a penalty. Another hard bugger was Ike Southward, the wingman at Workington. I remember going up there when Stan McCormick was the coach. In the dressing room before we kicked off Stan told us, 'Kick the ball over to Southward, he will not be able to do a thing, the bugger's older than me and has more strapping on him than Brian Bevan.' We did as we were told as the game started and kept kicking the ball to him in the first half. But we soon stopped that tactic just after he had scored his third try of the half. He was a player that took a lot of stopping as he proved that afternoon. He was a big fellow and deceptively quick and was hard to tackle and put on the ground.

I think we had one of the hardest wingmen playing at the time in Mick Sullivan. He had moved over from Wigan and was a very skilful player but people only seemed to think of him as a crash tackling machine. They tend to forget that he would often play at stand-off and could distribute the ball very well. Mick could come in off his wing and tackle the opposing centre just as he got the ball. His timing was superb. Mind you, it mattered not to Mick if you had the ball or not once he made his mind up to tackle you. When Mick hit you, you stayed hit. He was not the biggest player but he was feared throughout the game for his competitiveness and toughness. I never toured with him but those that did tell me he put the shits up more than one Aussie forward, let alone the three quarters, but he was also a great footballer.

Mick was also quite a character and I remember in one game at Hull when he had me in stitches. I never liked playing up at Hull as I did not like the spectators at the Boulevard. They used to sharpen the edge of a penny and then throw it at the players when they came near to the touchline. If you got tackled into touch by that old Threepenny Stand side of the ground, you got some abuse hurled at you; they would spit on you and call you all the names under the sun. We were playing there one afternoon and someone in the crowd in the Threepenny Stand threw an apple at Mick as he was standing on the touchline in a break in the play. As quick as a flash, Mick picked up the apple, wiped it clean on his shirt and proceeded to eat the bloody thing as he stood out on the wing. I bet the bloke that threw it was fuming. The rest of the Hull crowd in that stand voiced their anger but Mick just smiled, tossed the half eaten apple over the touchline, and carried on playing.

Whilst I was finding out about these players and learning the game I was also having a bit of success on the field when, in November 1961, we had won through to the Lancashire Cup Final and went out to play Swinton. It was a bit of an anti-climax after Wembley but I learned quickly that winning such finals was far more profitable than losing them. If we won then the following Thursday after training there would be a big fat bonus in our pay packets – taxed of course. If we lost then all we got was losing pay. It did help focus my mind because, after playing Rugby Union when winning or losing didn't matter so much, now losing a game hit me in the pocket!

We turned Swinton over that Saturday 25-9. We would meet them again in the same Final the following season but it was a lot closer at 7-4. I think we met Swinton three times in the Lancashire Cup Final and won all of them. I know it used to drive Albert Blan the Swinton skipper crazy that we always did them in cup matches. We also played Leigh and Oldham in the Final winning 15-4 and 30-2.

I played a lot against Blan and he was a bit of an oddity, an unlucky oddity at that. When we played Swinton, if he won the toss he would choose to play against the wind in the first half, and bugger me if the wind did not change round as half time approached so his team spent the whole game playing against the wind. He was not the fastest player, and I don't think I ever saw him sprint with the ball in his hand as that was not his game. He was a great organiser though, particularly when the four and then six-tackle rule came in as he was always one out from the ruck and would push a pass left or right. The thing was he had a lot of young players around him that ran onto the passes he sprayed out. But he just hated playing Saints in any sort of cup game as we always seemed to beat them, and he never seemed to make the right call whenever we tossed up.

The only time we had a struggle in the Lancashire Cup Final was in 1967 when we met Warrington. They had put together a strong squad and, in the first game in October, we actually drew 2-2. Back then if you drew the game it went to a replay, there was none of this extra time nonsense, or even worse the bloody 'golden point'. I believe that if the players have done their job and earned a draw, then it's an insult if they lose a game to a field goal in extra time. The problem in this case was that, due to fixture congestion, the replay did not take place until early in December and we had to raise our game once again. We managed to come away with a 13-10 win and I remember Harry Cook, one of our directors, sounded off in the paper after that final as only around 7,500 turned up to watch the game. He reckoned that it had cost the club money to win that cup. After their share of the gate and paying us winning money he claimed the club was out of pocket!

I played in five Lancashire Cup Finals and won all of them. However, it was the Challenge Cup back then which was the one everyone wanted to win. Having played in the 1961 Final I had to wait until 1966 before I got back there again but it was worth the wait I can tell you.

During that four or five years after I joined, the Saints team changed a great deal but we always seemed to have a good strong pack. We signed players like Bobby Wanbon, John Warlow, Ray French and John Mantle. John Warlow gave me one of the best laughs I have had on the rugby field when he got involved in a big brawl during the Challenge Cup semifinal against Dewsbury.

Frankie Barrow the full back, who always loved a bust up, must have run 80 yards to get involved in that one and we were all giving it a go when this woman suddenly climbed over the fence and ran on the field with an umbrella in her hand. She then started giving Dick Lowe, who John was battling with, a whacking with the umbrella she was carrying. It made the national papers and even the television. It turned out she was John's landlady and she had taken umbrage at 'her boy' being attacked. She was lead off the field by a policeman and Lowe took the umbrella and broke it in two he was so mad. I believe the rugby authorities banned her from all the grounds after that little episode. We gave John a bit of stick for months after that I can tell you.

I signed for Saints in December 1964 and, coming from Rugby Union, you could sometimes meet a great deal of resentment from players; after all they saw you as a big money signing. At Saints there was none of that and I went into the first team straight away, even though I had never played Rugby League. I have to say that Cliff was a colossus of a man; everyone knows how strong he was and how willing he was to do the hard stuff. It was a great advantage to have him in your team. He was also very quick for a prop forward but it used to upset him greatly that he could never catch me!

What people do not know is that Cliff was also a colossus off the field. He was a tremendous help to me when I moved up to St. Helens. I spent a great deal of time round at his house with his family and he became like a big brother to me. I knew well enough if someone took a swipe at me that, if I could not get them, then Cliff would make sure he did. He was a big believer in retribution – he never started the trouble but he sure did finish it.

St. Helens were a great team with some superb players

*but also a great family to belong to, and Cliff was at the
heart of it. Cliff in his prime had no equal anywhere in the
world in my opinion.*

John Mantle, St. Helens

We still had Tommy Voll playing with us but we had
also signed another South African, Len Killeen. While
I was with the club they seemed to sign a number of
Rugby Union players from South Africa, they brought
in Jan Prinsloo, Percy Lansburg, Ted Brophy and John
Gaydon who all contributed to our success. Of course
some did not make the grade. Killeen was different, he
came with a reputation as something of a goal kicker,
which was a bit of an understatement if ever there was
one. When Len was on form he could kick goals from in
the dressing room, the trouble was he could not tackle
a hot dinner. When he played, all I ever heard was this
bloody South African accent screaming out, 'Blind side
Cliff, blind side.' I had to do all his tackling as he was on
my side of the field.

I remember one Saturday going over to play
Blackpool who were not the best of teams. They had
signed Brian Bevan in an attempt to lift their gates and
he was playing on the wing that afternoon. I will never
forget Len looking down the field at this old man playing
against him thinking he was in for an easy afternoon.
We started the game and early in the first half we had
a scrum and Blackpool won the ball. By the time I had
got my head out of the scrum and I looked up, Bevan
was putting the ball down behind the sticks and Len
was looking totally bemused as to just how this old man
had got past him. As we were walking back toward our
line the referee said, 'Don't worry Lenny, he has scored

tries against better wingmen than you.' Len was fuming at that!

Mind you a bit later I was none too happy as I was marched for the first time in my career. Little Tommy Bishop, the Blackpool scrum-half, had given me a kick in the head while I was on the floor when the referee was elsewhere. I jumped up off the ground and tried to catch the little bugger but he was a bit too quick for me. The referee gave me a talking to and told me to get on with the game. Then Kenny Payne, the prop I was playing against that day who had been niggling me in the scrum right from the start of the game, had another go as we packed down again. I had had enough by then so I gave him one for his trouble and got a nice early bath while the rest of the lads carried on with the game.

But back to Len, who could kick goals like no one else. We were at Huddersfield one weekend and I was captaining the team. Huddersfield put it to us that afternoon and, on a cold, wet and windy day, they took the lead 5-0. We spent the rest of the game playing catch up but whenever we got into their 25 yard area, they simply took everything we threw at them. They tackled their hearts out and kept their try line intact. Later in the game we got a penalty out wide by the touchline. I told Len to put the ball in touch but he replied, 'No mate, I will kick the goal'. I thought he had no chance given the wet and windy conditions, but he insisted and blow me, if he didn't put it through the uprights. Then some minutes later the same thing happened, again out wide, and Len, refusing to follow my instructions, stuck the ball over the bar. Finally in the dying moments of the game, with the score at 5-4 to Huddersfield, we got another penalty 30 yards out on the touchline. Given the game was almost up, I didn't see any point in arguing with Len, then bugger me, into a swirling wind he went and did it again. We won that game 6-5 and it was all thanks to Len – and the fact that he refused to follow my instructions! Len always had confidence in his own ability with the boot as he demonstrated in the 1966 Challenge Cup Final when he argued with Alex Murphy, then simply slotted the ball through the posts from near the touchline, 65 yards out! He certainly was an amazing goal kicker.

*****

In that 1965-66 season we had a purple patch that lasted the whole campaign. I think at one stage we went about 22 games undefeated. We had got to the Championship Final at the end of the previous year only to get turned over by Halifax 15-7, which just made us more determined to not let it happen again. We won every cup that was available to win that year with the exception of one, The BBC Floodlit Trophy, when Castleford beat us 4-0.

Our 1965-66 Challenge Cup journey started at Wakefield in the first round. Back then they had a great side and Harold Poynton was their kingpin but we beat them 10-0. Our coach, Joe Coan, who confessed to never having played the game professionally so never tried to tell us how to play, made an exception that day. He took Peter Harvey, our young stand-off, to one side and said to him, 'I want you to follow Poynton all over the field. Wherever he goes I want you there with him. If he goes for a piss, I want you with him in the bloody toilet.' Young Peter did just that and for 80 minutes whenever

Poynton got the ball, he got Peter at the same time. Peter just snuffed him out of the game.

In the next round we had to play Swinton who we always seemed to put one over in cup ties. We went into the game feeling confident and put them away 16-4.

In round three we had to up our game as Hull KR gave us a hell of a scrap and we only just secured a 12-10 win. That set up a semifinal match against Dewsbury who had been having a good cup run, but we were so fit we always believed we could beat them. That was due to Joe who was a fitness training fanatic. The fitness work wasn't something we enjoyed, but it certainly helped with all the extra cup games that season and we ran out 12-5 victors over Dewsbury to set up a Wembley Final meeting with arch-rivals Wigan.

Our extra fitness work had come about back in the winter of 1962 to 63 when Stan McCormick was the coach. That winter the weather turned bitterly cold and the country suffered a big freeze. No one could train or play as the grounds were all frozen solid for weeks on end. To keep us active, we started training at the gym in the school where future coach Joe taught. Through that winter, while every other bugger was playing darts and dominos, we were climbing up and down ropes and all sorts of other silly stuff. It was this that first brought Joe to the attention of the board and when they were looking for a new coach, having decided to part company with McCormick, they remembered the good work Joe had done in the big freeze. Joe really did get us fit and it was something he maintained once he got the coaching job. So when we got back to the Final in 1966, the fitness we had built up under Joe gave us confidence that we could turn Wigan over, just like back in the 1961 Final.

The club really wanted success in the Challenge Cup that season because they took us into camp before the semifinal, which was something that normally only happened once you won through to the Final. I think we were in a hotel in Hale. It had an atrium so that each floor could see down to the foyer. We were all on the third floor and I remember Tommy Bishop, who had recently joined us from Blackpool via Barrow, was getting a bit uppity one time, as only scrum halves can, so Ray French and myself grabbed him and we each held a leg and hung him over the balcony. Poor Tommy nearly shit himself.

I remember Cliff and Ray dangling me over the balcony all too bloody well. I was a cheeky little bugger and Cliff was so strong he simply picked me up and hung me over the side and did about three press ups with me hanging in thin air. He asked me if I was going to give it a rest or should he let me go. I am not sure if he really would have dropped me but I decided not to find out.

Tommy Bishop, St. Helens and Cronulla

The hotel we were in was supposedly haunted. The story was that a number of shipwrecked sailors were put up in the second floor rooms and some lunatic came in and stabbed them all. I know Frenchy was terrified once he found it was haunted. A few years later they knocked the place down and the Irish lads who were doing the demolition would not sleep in the place. One of the men had a dog which was happy to run around the place but was terrified of going on to the second floor. I got a phone call from Frenchy when he read the story about the Irish dog in the local newspaper telling me, 'I told you the place was bloody haunted.'

I was much better prepared for the second Wembley game than the first, and better able to appreciate the whole event. Also I was one of the elder statesmen in the side as I think there was only Murphy, Tommy Voll and myself left from the team that had won in 1961. In the run up to the Final, Wigan had a bit of strife. Colin Clarke, their hooker who had replaced Bill Sayer when he joined Saints, had been sent off and was to face the disciplinary. I think everyone felt that he would not get suspended, but sadly he did and missed the Final. We had one of the best hookers around at the time with Bill and Wigan did not have a reserve hooker of his quality. They roped in their prop, Tommy Woosey, as a makeshift hooker.

Having got to the Final, we once again went into camp, but this time we stayed at The Queens Hotel in Southport, which I thought was a lucky omen as Barbara and I had spent our honeymoon there. Coan told us that we could have all the eggs, milk, vegetables and steak we wanted but no chips or potatoes and we took him at his word. Frenchy, Killeen, Albert Halsall, Billy Benyon and I could pack the stuff away. We would order a couple of sirloin steaks with all the veggies and clean the plate. The hotel had a little Palm Court type orchestra and one of the band members used to work in the Army Catering Corps and he was amazed at the amount of food we scoffed. He said to me, 'I have fed soldiers coming back from days out on manoeuvres who could not shift the stuff you lads have got through.' I hate to think what the bill was for the club but we just filled our boots for a few days.

While we were at the hotel, I decided to put the wind up Frankie Barrow. I waited until it was around midnight and then scrambled out of my bedroom window on the third floor, made my way along the edge of the building until I got to Frankie's room and then banged on the window. It scared the life out of him, I thought he was going to pass out from sheer fright. It was those sorts of things that always went on amongst the lads that added to the camaraderie.

One afternoon we all went down to the boating lake and got into the rowing boats. I had a cine camera with me and spent a great deal of time watching my team-mates try to sink the boat Warlow and Frenchy were in. I am not sure just why those two were targeted but we chased the buggers all over the lake. Many years later, when they were having a surprise 60th birthday party for Ray, I sent over the film of him in the boat working like hell just to stay afloat as he came under attack from the rest of us. It was incidents like that which took our minds off the Final and helped us to relax.

When I think about it, there seemed to be a great many incidents that involved my good mate Frenchy, but then he could be the life and soul of the party at times. While we were in camp before Wembley we had the restaurant to ourselves and some of the lads did a 'turn' one evening. Frenchy and I arranged to put a screen up in the middle of the dance floor from which he would appear. When Frenchy got up on the dance floor he was wearing only a jock strap, some plastic flowers – that we had taken from the plant pots around the place – and a couple of silk scarves that he had borrowed from the receptionist. He started to perform a striptease to the tune 'Hot Diggity'. I was by the door to the ballroom and, as he got to the interesting bit, quick as a flash I opened the door and started to usher in a group of old age pensioners I'd seen milling around outside. Frenchy's face was a picture and the rest of the lads simply fell about laughing. He certainly got more applause than he was anticipating!

One of the traditions associated with getting to Wembley is the team photograph and, as we prepared for ours, I could not help but think back to the last Wembley photo in 1961. Back then Vince Karalius and Don Vines were like cat and dog, they could not agree what bloody day it was. The club decided that they would photograph us in our Wembley outfit, which was a blazer and slacks. We were all given a red rose to wear in our lapel for the occasion. Now Vines was based in Yorkshire and he turned up for the photograph wearing a white jacket; he had his Wembley blazer but was wearing the white coat simply to wind Vince up and it worked. I thought Vince was about to kill him. Vince was never a pretty sight, but a mad Vince was bloody fearsome. We had to keep the two buggers apart as best we could until game time.

When we went down to London, I was better able to appreciate just how important this Final was, not just to the players but the supporters. Also we knew that there would probably be a full house at Wembley with 100,000 being allowed to watch, whereas back in 1961, the limit was 95,000. I am sure that they shut Wigan and St. Helens for that Saturday as it seemed like the entire populations of both towns were inside the stadium. I enjoyed all the pre-match build up this time and when we walked out I was able to look around and enjoy the sight of almost 100,000 screaming fans.

I know that people thought the match was spoiled as a spectacle because of the rules that were in place at that time. If a player strayed offside, the opposition, from their penalty, had to kick to touch and then a scrum was set. Because Clarke the hooker was missing from the Wigan team, we won almost every scrum, but contrary to common belief we did not need to keep going offside to give away a penalty. The truth was that Wigan never really touched the bloody ball all the game. Once we got it we simply kept it, and when Wigan did get a sniff of the ball, one of our lads would eventually go offside when we got fed up with tackling.

I do remember the game simply flew past, just as the last time, and was over before I knew it. Killeen loved being in the limelight, he was a big game player, the bigger the game the better he performed. About 10 minutes in we were already two points up when we got that penalty five yards inside our own half. Len was pumped up and pointing to the sticks as he was talking to Alex and I knew he was in the mood for having a dig. I remembered the Huddersfield game but even I thought he had no chance as the Wembley stadium seemed so vast. But true to form, Len booted the ball right over the bar for two points. It mattered not how far out that the kick was, Len always seemed to take that little run up of his and give the ball one hell of a whack. A little later Len stepped up again to slot yet another two pointer over and we were 6-0 up. And while Len seemed to be able to do no wrong with the boot, Laurie Gilfedder for Wigan was off target that afternoon and missed a couple of sitters.

About 20 minutes in, John Mantle gave us our first try having been sent on his way from a pass by Tommy Voll. Killeen, of course, added the conversion to take us 9-0 up, but Gilfedder added two points for Wigan from a penalty a few minutes later

In the second half we continued where we left off and, about 15 minutes in, we were attacking when Benyon put in a perfectly weighted grubber kick from about 10 yards out. Killeen was quickest to react, gathered the ball and dived in to score in the corner. Then just to prove me wrong, he missed bloody the conversion! Following that we were nearly home and hosed. Tommy Voll had a try disallowed in the corner but Bishop scored our third try after collecting his own kick which had, luckily, bounced off a Wigan player's leg; Killeen converting to take the score to 19-2. Then in the dying seconds, Murphy dropped a goal to put the icing on the cake and make the result 21-2.

I will never forget the look on Sayer's face as the final whistle went. He felt that he had got one over his old team and his smile was so big his face disappeared. The other thing I remember is that Frenchy had a terrific game that afternoon. He was all over that pitch and tackled anything that moved, in fact I think he tackled me three bloody times that day! He must have been in the running for the Lance Todd Trophy but in the end they gave it to Killeen for his spectacular goal kicking and his try.

After the match the press gave us a hard time, claiming the game had been spoiled as a spectacle by our tactics in forcing Wigan to scrum, but we had the cup for our efforts and Wigan did not. However, in the close season, the league officials voted 21-2 to change the rule allowing a tap restart from an offside penalty but it came too late for Wigan.

For me the Final was much more satisfying than the first time, simply because I was more experienced and more aware of the importance of the occasion. The problem was that after the game we did celebrate, but we had a Championship Final to play the following Saturday, so we couldn't really go overboard. I also wasn't celebrating on the following Thursday when I picked up my pay packet. We had been on a bonus of £100 to win at Wembley and £12 if we lost but, when I opened my packet, I think I had a fiver at most in it. I had bought tickets for most of my family to watch the game and of course they never paid for them. So for beating Wigan at Wembley I took home £5!

We knew that after the Wembley Final we had to play Halifax in the Championship Final we also knew they had beaten us in the same Final the previous season. Sure we had a drink or two but it was not like today with silly bloody Mad Mondays. In any case, we were only part-time professional and had to be back at work first thing on Monday morning. Also I think we respected ourselves and our team-mates more back then. If you celebrated too much on the piss, and it resulted in your performance being poor the next game, then not only had you let yourself down but also your team-mates, and in my day that was unforgivable. Mind you, at the time I did not drink. I had enjoyed a pint whilst playing Union but one night I drank a pint that was 'off' and was as sick as a dog. I could never face drinking beer after that.

The other thing was that we could not let our hair down too much as we had been invited to appear on TV on *The Eamonn Andrews Show* on the Saturday night along with the Challenge Cup. Muhammad Ali was also on the show, and in the corridor before the show started Ali began winding us up wanting us to prove how tough we really were. I thought I am not having all this shit, so

I threw a rugby ball down the corridor to him and asked him to run it back at me. I told him we would see how tough he was after a short arm tackle. Last thing I saw of him was when his minders ushered him away to safety!

On the Sunday after the Final and our television appearance, we caught the train up to Liverpool and boarded an open-topped bus from the station right to Knowsley Road. The streets were lined with thousands of supporters and it's only when you experience something like that that you realise just how important winning a Wembley Final is and just how much the supporters want it. It seemed like the whole of St. Helens had turned out to line the streets to see us and it made for a very special day.

At training after Wembley, Coan was aware that we couldn't relax and told us that we needed to raise our game again for the Championship Final. Often after winning a trophy a team can go through a bit of a slump, but at that time the Saints team was like one big family, and we all got on so well that we didn't want to let each other down. In fact we probably spent more time together than we actually did with our own families with all the matches and training. And we were determined to avenge the defeat to Halifax the previous year when we lined up against them again in the Championship Final at Swinton on the Saturday.

That 1966 Championship involved the top 16 clubs in a series of play-offs to get to the Final. We had ended the season at the top of the ladder, winning 28 games and drawing one. We then had to go through the rigmarole of playing the team that had finished in 16th spot. We played Warrington and hammered them 35-7, and followed that up by knocking over Oldham 15-10 and then Hull KR 14-6 to get to the Final. On that Saturday we went over to Station Road at Swinton without Tommy Voll who was not fit to play. If our supporters were worried at losing him, they need not have bothered. That afternoon, in front of over 30,000 supporters, we played even better than we had at Wembley and prop Halsall had the proverbial blinder. Albert could run like the wind for a prop, simply because he had started out as a wingman.

The match started with Halifax scoring from a penalty followed by an unconverted try from Killeen. Halifax then added a try from Terry Fogerty which they converted to put the score at 3-7. After that it was one-way traffic with Halsall scoring two tries, Killeen a goal and a penalty and Murphy a drop goal to take us in at half time 15-7 up.

In the second half a big brawl kicked off on the pitch with most of the players involved, and a lady from St. Helens came out of the crowd and started belting the bloody Halifax players with her handbag. But it made no difference as we finished Halifax off and gained our revenge with a try from Barrow and two more from Killeen. Halifax scored a consolation try and goal in the dying seconds but we had the game in the bag by then and won 35-12.

Halsall deservedly won the Harry Sunderland Trophy for his man-of-the-match performance and we finished the season winning everything, with the exception of the BBC Floodlit Trophy.

*****

After that double-winning season, the team went through a rebuilding stage, although the pack seemed to remain as strong as ever. Also the repercussions of the Wembley Final saw the rules change allowing a tap from an offside penalty. But even more radical was the ending of unlimited tackles and introduction of the four-tackle rule. That took a bit of getting used to but we seemed to do as well as most other clubs in that department. I will say this about the four-tackle rule, when it was introduced it ruined the careers of many players, particularly the big slow front row forwards in the game, and at Saints it proved to be the end for Albert Halsall.

It was really quite funny the way Albert joined the club. He was playing for Salford at the time and we actually played them in a League game. Unfortunately Albert and I had a sort of disagreement over something and nothing and it degenerated into a bit of a scrap. The referee was not happy and the result was we both went for an early bath. The following Tuesday we were both at the disciplinary as a result, awaiting our fate. On the Thursday at training Harry Cook said to me, 'Cliff we have just signed a front row forward to play with you and Bill Sayer in the pack.' I asked who it was only to be told it was Albert. I thought, bloody hell that's a turn up for the books, but I was happy to have him on my side hitting the opposition rather than hitting me.

Sadly after doing so well for the club in that first season, the rule getting rid of the unlimited tackles did for Albert. I remember talking to him on many an occasion and he said the same thing every time, 'I cannot cope with this, we get the ball and four tackles later we have to kick and then have a scrum. Are there not enough bloody scrums in the game already?' I told him that we all had to adapt, I was not a ball-playing front row, I was simply a head-down, arse-up, take the ball forward type of player and the game would always want players who could and would do that.

Unfortunately Albert could not or would not adapt, and the daft thing is that he was such a good player he could well have gone on tour in 1966. I remember he had been selected in the Great Britain training squad and I was supposed to pick him up on the East Lancs Road at St. Helens to go over to Leeds for training. He never turned up and I drove over the hill to training on my own. When I got there and they asked where he was, I tried to cover for him saying I did not know where he was but he had been suffering from a touch of flu. Back then there were no mobile phones to check up on him and, having missed the training session, he was never asked back and so missed out on selection for that tour in my opinion.

One thing in particular I do remember about that season was travelling over to play Liverpool City. In the dressing room I saw what I thought was a large tin of Vaseline and, as was my usual trick, I proceeded to rub it all over my back and private parts. Frenchy sat there laughing at me and I could not figure out why, but I soon found out as what I thought was Vaseline turned out to be wintergreen. I spent the whole of the coach's pre-match talk leaning over the wall of the big bath in the dressing room with Ray hosing me down with cold water. I was even running on the spot at half time. Frenchy said to me after the game, 'You ran around like a man on fire, boy you played a blinder'. I think he was getting his own back on me for the 'Hot Diggity' affair at Southport.

We went on to finish in fourth spot on the ladder at the end of the season, and in the top 16 play-off we beat first Leigh then Bradford over at Odsal, and then went to Castleford and turned them over to get to the Championship Final for the third season on the trot. In that Final we actually fought out a 7-7 draw against Wakefield Trinity in front of 20,000 fans at Headingley. I think drawing a final is nearly as bad as losing one. You have given 80 minutes and have nothing to show for it other than the thought of going through the same rigmarole for another 80 minutes. Mind you, I still believe it is the best way to settle a game rather than the extra time or golden point rubbish. We actually played the replay on the Wednesday at Swinton and over 33,500 turned up to watch. Sadly we did not really perform in that game and Wakefield took the title winning 21-9. When Super League goes on about The Theatre of Dreams crap, everyone seems to forget just how much of a draw the game was for fans back in the 1960s. Pre Super League many games would draw over 30,000 through the turnstiles, but you would think that never happened if you listen to the folks on Sky Sports.

The following season we again finished in fourth place, but in the play-off we lost in the semifinal to Hull KR. In the 1968-69 campaign, we managed to win the Lancashire Cup once again, beating Oldham quite easily in the Final by a score of 30-2. However, that year Castleford seemed to become the monkey on our back. In previous seasons we had always seemed to be able to get the better of them, but that season they turned the table big style.

Having won the Lancashire Cup we felt that we could

well be in for another trophy haul. In the Challenge Cup we got out of gaol in one of the early rounds when we just managed to scrape a 4-4 draw against Doncaster, but we learned from that and won the replay with ease 36-0. We got to the semifinal of the cup and played Castleford who beat us that afternoon 6-3. The misery for us did not end there as at the end of the season we had finished second and once again won through to the Championship semifinal. Once again we faced Castleford and once again they did us, but this time far easier 18-6.

I was a bit fed up at the end of that campaign but come the 1969-70 season we were all raring to go, and I was pleased and privileged to captain the side. One of the things I did on becoming captain was to ask the players to agree to a scheme I had. In the John Player Cup games and the likes, a man of the match was selected and they got a little trophy and a bit of cash. I suggested that the cash prize be split with half going to the player and the other half to a kitty to be used to fund a trip away at the end of the season. The players agreed and we set it up but the problem was that most of the prize money seemed to be won by Kel Coslett. He was the player kicking goals and scoring tries, so I suppose it was only to be expected, but he was not best pleased at funding our end of season trip.

At the season's end we duly went away but it was a far cry from the Mad Monday exploits of today's players – we had a night out in a dance hall in Southport! I do remember that on the way home from Southport one of the lads, Bobby Blackwood, got a bit uppity so we turfed him off and made him jog behind the coach for a mile or two just to let him know what was what.

There was one game in that season that I am very proud to have been involved in, especially as captain. It was made very clear to me early in my career at Saints that you can forget Wembley finals or international caps as only two games are important to the club and the supporters. They were Wigan at Knowsley Road and Wigan at Central Park. You could lose every other game but those two had to be won at all costs. On Boxing Day 1969, we went over to Central Park for the traditional derby game and walked off the field winners by 53 points to 11. It was a record score against Wigan and I was privileged to score two tries that day. I remember walking back after we had scored a try and seeing the Wigan fans walking out of the ground in disgust and thinking, bloody hell there must still be half an hour to go yet! Mind you, the buggers did us when we played them at home winning 23-16.

We finished in third spot at the end of that season but we failed to make any great inroads in the Challenge Cup. Then in the top 16 play-offs we suffered a bout of déjà vu as we had to face Castleford in yet another semifinal. It turned out to be a close affair and at the end of 80 minutes we could not be separated with the scores locked at 9-9. In the replay it was our turn to get the monkey off our backs and we beat them 21-12, setting up a meeting with Leeds in the Final.

The Final was held on May 16th at Odsal and the Leeds team, who were packed with big-name stars, were favourites for the trophy. However, we had an ace in the pack as Frank Myler had joined us that season from Widnes and he played a blinder that day. Also because Leeds had rangy wingers in John Atkinson and Alan Smith, our new coach Cliff Evans (Joe Coan had left by then) selected Eric Prescott on the wing in place of Frank Wilson who had been there all season. Eric was a strong, fast, powerful player so his job was to stop any raids down the wing. A lot of people thought Cliff was mad as Wilson was our top scorer at the time. But with Wilson, when he was good, he was very good but it depended a lot on which Wilson turned up on the day.

Leeds opened the scoring with a try from Smith but we got one back when Sayer crossed the line. The game then went back and forth and we went in at half time trailing 8-7. In the second half we came out fired up and turned them over. Prescott scored two tries – the first was a beauty as we moved the ball from player to player – and Walsh added another. We ran out easy winners in the end 24-12, and Myler deservedly picked up the Harry Sunderland Trophy

I remember going up to collect the cup which is a great, big thing with ornate handles. There is a great picture which made the newspapers of myself and Coslett holding the cup up and I have my finger stuck in the bloody handle. I had put my finger through a hole and could not get it out. Kel was laughing his head off and I thought I was going to have to take the cup home with me.

It was during that season that the use of substitutions had also changed. We had been able to make substitutions up until half time, which was mainly used to replace injured players until that season, but we were now allowed to use subs through the whole game for the first time. After that rule change, coaches used the subs to make tactical changes rather than replacing injured players. That's evolved into the bloody ridiculous situation in the game today with players running on and off all the time. Nowadays if a prop is not on the field he is sitting on the side line pedalling a bloody bike. What is that all about? I would have found the bike riding more tiring than actually playing the game. Props do not play 80 minutes these days, they seem to play just two 20 minute stints. It has taken the need for stamina out of the game. You can go on the field and run around like a madman for 20 minutes knowing that you are going to get 30 or even 50 minutes to recover before going back on again. That is bloody daft; in my mind a game lasts 80 minutes and players should play for 80 minutes unless they are injured.

*****

The 1970-71 season proved to be my last for St. Helens and moves were under way for me to go and play down under, but more of that later. I was still captaining the side and we were playing consistently. In December we reached the Floodlit Trophy Final, but Leeds got their revenge for the Championship Final as they won 9-5 at Headingley.

At the end of the season we finished second, and in the top 16 play-offs we had an easy run beating Huddersfield and then Hull to take us into the semifinal to face Leeds. Unfortunately in the semi I went in to make a tackle and, as my hand was on a Leeds players' knee and my elbow was on his other knee, John Mantle came in and hit the player with a tackle and his knees hit my outstretched forearm at the same time and broke my arm. We beat Leeds in that game to go through to the Final to face Wigan at Swinton's Station Road ground.

We won the Final 16-12 but unfortunately I wasn't in the team that put one over our arch rivals as the broken arm had ended my season.

After the Final the team went over to France, and because I was club captain the board took me with them, so I went with my arm in plaster. The club also invited Sayer who was ending his time at Saints and Dagnall who had retired a few years earlier, to make the trip over to Perpignan. It was quite ironic that when I first decided to try my luck with Saints my arm was in plaster, and then when I left the club my arm was in plaster. I had done 11 years with the club and the time was right for me to move on to pastures new. But what I thought was perhaps the end turned out to be the new beginning.

Though the mildest and most warm-hearted of men off the field, Cliff was, and still is, one of the hardest, toughest and most resilient forwards I have ever played alongside, against or watched through my 50 years in professional Rugby League. Cliff was the 'rock' up front who set the example for all and helped to induce such a mentality and work rate amongst the forwards. There was certainly no relaxing when Cliff, so fit and strong, was leading from the front.

Nor was there any slacking by the likes of myself when sitting alongside him as he was enjoying any of the pre-match meals which used to accompany all of our away matches. Not for Cliff the diet of the modern player, prepared by the club's dietician and the counting of calories and carbohydrates. During a large four-course meal, my steak pie or apple pie and custard frequently disappeared from off my plate unless I constantly kept a fork in them. His appetite matched his energy and strength on the field. And such was the warmth of his companionship, friendship and support to all of our team, and especially to myself, that he helped to foster the unique team spirit we had with St. Helens.

Ray French

*****

I think at this point I should refute one issue that people think of me. Contrary to popular belief, I got on quite well with referees in England, but down under was a different story. Most of the referees treated the players with respect and I did the same with them, and I have to say that some of them were quite humorous when they refereed the game.

On one occasion – I think it was an international against France – Eric 'Sergeant-Major' Clay was in charge and he blew up and gave a penalty against Alex Murphy. True to form Alex disagreed, and ran off cursing and swearing at Clay. So the referee blew his whistle again and called out, 'Come here Yappy'. Now when it came to verbals, Alex could hold his own with anyone, so as he approached Clay he said, 'You can't call me that, you have to call me by my number or by my position.' Not to be outdone the referee replied, 'Oh a smart-arse are we? Well we better get the captain over.' On that afternoon, the captain was the great Eric Ashton, and on listening to both Clay and Alex he pointed out that Alex was right and he should be addressed correctly. Clay looked at the pair of them and said, 'I have a long memory,' and with that he sent them back to get on with the game. That proved to be the case because, a couple of weeks after that game, Wigan and Saints played in the local derby. Clay was again the referee and when Eric Ashton and Alex Murphy got into a bit of a 'blue', which was unusual from Eric as that was never his thing, Clay blew up and called them both over. After talking to them he sent the pair of them off with the words as they left the field, 'I told you I had a long memory.'

There was another ref whose name was Joe Manley and the players nicknamed him 'Play on Joe.' because he hated to stop the game for an infringement. We were playing in a Floodlit Trophy game and true to form I shouted to him, 'Joe that pass was a mile forward.' As he was running past me he shouted as he always did, 'Play on Cliff, play on.' During that game we had the most officious linesman in the around at the time. I think he used to starch his underpants as well as his flag as nothing was ever out of place. He was forever running on the pitch with his flag up, so I finally said to Joe, 'The bugger is on again Joe.' Sure enough he was stood on the playing surface with his flag in the air. Joe called both captains over and told us to listen to the touch judge's report. When he had finished Joe said to him, 'Now listen, I have the whistle and you have the bloody flag, now bugger off the field and don't come on again.'

On another occasion we went to play Liverpool and it was a freezing cold afternoon with the rain bucketing down. The pitch was a quagmire and no one wanted to play. Our captain at the time, Vince Karalius, said to the referee, Charlie Appleton, 'Come on Charlie, surely we are not going to play in this?' Charlie replied that we would start the game and after 60 minutes he would abandon the match and the result would stand. We played the first half and we were all freezing as we went out for the second 40 minutes and as we were playing

Vince kept shouting, 'Come on Charlie, blow the whistle, we are freezing out here. 'Just give it another five minutes Vince,' would come the reply. Eventually he did blow for time and Vince went up to him and said, 'Did we get the 60 minutes in Charlie?' Charlie Appleton with a broad grin on his face told Vince we had played the 80 minutes and he had conned us all. I cannot tell you what Vince had to say!

It was only when I became captain that I really began to think about the referees, mainly because I would need to speak to them to ask what a penalty was for and so on. I could not tell you most of the time who had refereed a game. If you could not remember the referee's name then in my opinion he had done his job as people came to watch Rugby League and not a referee blowing up all the time. When I was captain I would see who was the referee was and give the players guidance such as, 'Be careful, this guy likes a clean play the ball,' or, 'You can get away with a bit in the scrums.' But on the whole I had a great deal of respect for the British referees. However, the referees in Australia were another story and, having had run-ins with them while on tour, I was about to have to deal with them on a weekly basis for the next part of my career.

When you play the game as a professional, I suppose it is only natural to develop a liking for your own home ground. There is a familiarity about it that seems to settle players down and they become comfortable in their surroundings. I was just the same. I loved playing at Knowsley Road but there were other grounds that I used to like travelling to. I liked going over to Central Park and also over to Headingley. They were great stadiums with a superb atmosphere. I always thought that Workington had a good playing surface, one of the best. Whitehaven, on the other hand, was not my favourite ground that is for sure.

We travelled up to play Whitehaven one Saturday as the rain came down steadily until we reached Keswick, and then from there on it pissed down non-stop. We got to the ground fully expecting the game to be called off but we were amazed when the ref said it was playable. He did say that if the surface cut up he would abandon the game after 60 minutes so the result would stand. I thought the pitch had cut up before we even kicked off, but we played the game and Whitehaven scored a try and kicked the goal which sticks in my mind because it was kicked into the teeth of a gale to put us 5-0 down. We dug in and Kel Coslett managed to kick a couple of goals to get us back in the game. You could not tell who was who as we all looked the same covered in mud, so what the fans thought God only knows.

In the second half Coslett put us in front with his third goal which seemed to upset the Whitehaven lads who thought they could turn us over. Halfway through that second half there was an almighty scrap and every one piled in. Back then when such things happened the ref and touch judges would run in and start to haul players off and try to settle the situation down. Unfortunately that afternoon, as the referee ran in to try and calm everybody down, he copped an elbow right in the mouth for his troubles. The thing was he had his whistle in it at the time and it smashed his front teeth out. He could not continue and, as neither of the two touch judges were qualified to referee a first grade game, the match was abandoned. The problem was at the time of the abandonment we had only played around 59 and a half minutes. Later the Whitehaven club demanded a replay which, thank God, they did not get and the result stood.

We tramped off the pitch through the mud which was at least a foot deep in places, we were soaking wet as the rain had not relented all though the match. We must have been carrying two stone extra with the mud stuck to us and the rain that had soaked into the cotton jerseys – we did not have the benefit of the modern materials the shirts are made from nowadays. When we arrived at the dressing room, Len Killeen was prancing about as happy as a sandboy with hardly a mark on his shirt. I looked at him and asked him what was up and when he spoke I realised he was 'half cut'. It seems that as the game had been a forward battle, he really had nothing to do, and in an attempt to keep the cold out he kept nipping over the touchline to the dugout and having a drink of brandy from Joe Coan's flask. He was as pissed as a newt by the time the game was called off!

Funnily enough I never seemed to get the same affinity with Aussie grounds once I moved down under that I did with those back home. There were grounds you loved to go to and others you hated visiting but it was not the same in Sydney. I think a lot of that was due to the fact that the supporters were so far from the action that the players did not feel there was any atmosphere.

The one ground I never liked playing at was Batley. At their Mount Pleasant ground you had to walk through the crowd to get onto the pitch, and that bloody slope was a killer. Batley would always try to get down into that bottom right hand corner of the ground where it was difficult for the opposition to get out of if Batley lost the ball. They actually used to work a set move once they got into that corner that involved their prop, Trevor Eastwood, coming through onto a short pass. Eastwood was a nuggety prop forward who was not very tall. I called him 'Oddjob' and he was a tough little bugger I can tell you. I think he was responsible for one of my broken arms, or at least his head was as I caught him across the forehead with my forearm, not the cleverest thing I've ever done and which resulted in another three hour wait in casualty.

Another who had a hard head was a prop named Worthy who played for Keighley. The first time I broke my arm we were playing Keighley at home and I think we were winning quite easily at the time. Then as Worthy came running through I lined him up, but as I got to him he slipped and I short armed him right across the forehead and at the same time I followed through with my shoulder. He was in Disneyland before he hit the floor and I was thinking that was a good hit – that was until I looked down and saw my hand seemed to be the wrong way round! It is really strange when you break a bone because your body seems automatically to let the broken limb go to the most comfortable position, I suppose to lessen the pain. It is only when you try to move the arm that you get the pain, and when the physio tried to move my hand, boy did I know about it.

They took me straight to hospital to have my arm reset and as they were doing it I said to the young doctor, 'I think you had better ring Mr. Herron'. He was the specialist who looked after the Saints players. The doctor looked at me with fear in his eyes saying that he could not disturb Mr. Herron with a trivial thing like a simple broken arm. We continued the conversation until I finally said, 'Look doc, one of us is going to get their arse kicked by Mr. Herron if he finds out he has not been contacted, and it is not going to be me.' Eventually the young doctor relented and plucked up the courage to ring Mr. Herron who told him exactly what he should do and to call him back once the arm had been reset and the x-ray showed it was in the right place. The other thing about that break was that it cost me a place in the team against Leigh in the Lancashire Cup Final!

When I eventually got to see Mr. Herron a few weeks later and the arm was mended, he said to me, 'I would like you to wear this when you play,' and pulled out this arm guard. It was made from plastic and fitted over my forearm. I laughed my head off and told him I couldn't wear it as it would be a lethal weapon on the field so no referee would allow it. I think he was a little disappointed that his toy was not going to get a run out. The other thing I remember about Mr. Herron was that when I was at Cronulla and Tommy Bishop snapped his Achilles tendon, he came home to get it repaired and went to see Mr. Herron who sewed the tendon back together. Given the time it had taken to get back to the UK for the operation, they thought Tommy would struggle to walk properly again, never mind play rugby. It tells you how good Mr. Herron was as Tommy captained Cronulla in the Grand Final a year later!

3

An International

I can still remember the day when I really started my rugby career with Dudley Kingswinford. It was Saturday September 24th, 1955 and I was just 15 years and six months old when I played for the newly formed colts side. During my career in Rugby Union I turned out for the club 96 times and scored nine tries. I did not think too much about it at the time, but I must have had a bit of speed as I was selected to play for the club in three seven-a-side competitions. When I was 20 I was lucky enough to win selection as a prop for Worcester and Herefordshire combined counties and actually played three games for the counties. I realise that while my club was a junior club, the county side was also a junior set up, albeit at a slightly higher level. It could not be compared with the likes of Lancashire or Yorkshire back then. We were never going to provide players for the England international team. I was aware that I had probably reached the height of my representative career in the game. I played a total of 115 games in the Union code before signing as a professional with Saints.

When I started playing Rugby League, the thought of actually playing international rugby never entered my head; it was never on my radar. I was more concerned with firstly learning the game, secondly trying to get into the first team and thirdly, having got a first team place keeping the bloody thing. Little did I know that a little over a year after signing as a pro I was to sample international Rugby League. True I was playing for Saints, one of the big teams in the game, but on October 14th, 1961, only 14 months after switching codes, I ran out onto the pitch at Knowsley Road and our opponents were the New Zealand tourists. I was 21 and, to be honest, I never had any fear of the opposition. I was playing with a team of international or ex-international players so we were never going to be out-classed. With the exception of myself and Brian McGinn the rest were internationals in the side. The senior players did not throw the likes of me a novice newcomer to the wolves, they guided and taught me how to play the game. We actually knocked New Zealand over that day 25-10, I know that Tommy Voll scored one and both the youngsters, McGinn and Keith Northey, got a try and the pack chipped in with a try from Abe Terry and Dick Huddart. I thought I would like some more of this but I had to wait a couple of seasons before I got another taste.

In 1963 the Aussies came over, and at the end of September they came to Knowsley Road and only just got the better of us that afternoon by 8-2. I was the type of player that did not worry about the opposition, I just went out there and did the best that I could every game. I remember during the game that Tommy Voll got the ball and when he got tackled, the Aussies, who had obviously heard about him, decided to rough him up. Now that was something you did not do. In many respects Tommy was our meal ticket, he could win a game on his own and put winning pay in our pockets, so we always looked after him. I saw what was happening and ran in and got involved in a scrap with a couple of the Aussies. I am not sure if it was that set-to that first brought me to the attention of the international selectors or not, but they must have seen that I was not frightened of the tourists and was not prepared to take a backward step. More importantly, I was prepared to take anyone on that had a go at one of my team-mates.

I am perhaps one of only a few players who managed to play in a club side that beat the touring Australian side twice. When the Aussies came back we actually turned them over 8-4 in a nasty ill-tempered affair. I remember that Billy Benyon took a bit of stick and decided to dish a bit out himself. The result was that both he and the Aussie forward he had a disagreement with got an early bath. The next time the tourists came to Knowsley Road we really did for them and gave them a 37-10 hammering. That did not go down well with the Aussies I can tell you. I got a bit of stick as during the game I tackled John Coote, or should I say Father John Coote as he was a priest, and he got a broken nose as a result. Certainly as a result of that game there were one or two players waiting for me when I moved down under.

When the Ashes series of 1963 began, the first Test was played down in London at Wembley and I was not selected. In truth I did not expect to be, I was not into that mode of thinking. At that time I had no pretensions that I was an international prop, but the Aussies ran riot that day beating us easily 28-2 and so changes were expected to be made to the team. I got the shock of my life when the call came that I had been selected to play against the tourists in the second Test. I didn't really believe it, even when I saw the team printed in the newspaper for the Game at Swinton. The team that day was: Gower, Sullivan, Ashton, Fox, Stopford, Myler,

Murphy, Robinson, McIntyre, Watson, Measures, Morgan, Karalius.

When we kicked off in the second Test, we started well and I think we were 8-0 up, but then we suffered a couple of injuries and players had to leave the field. First we lost Myler with a rib injury and then the captain, Ashton, could not come out for the second half as he also picked up a rib injury. Substitutions were something for the future then and we had to shift players around. We had second-row forwards on the wing and we simply did not have enough pace out wide to hold the Aussies once they started moving the ball about and we lost the game 50-12 in the end.

What brassed me off, and has done for 50 years, was that the Aussie press referred to that game as the finest performance by an Australian side ever! They very conveniently forget to mention that we played the whole of the second half with only 11 men and also a part of the first half with Myler off and Ashton a passenger. Eventually the true story was told in the November 2013 issue of the *Men of League* magazine here in Australia. In that issue they actually wrote that England only had 11 on the pitch for most of the game. I am a member of the Men of League Foundation and actually rang the magazine editor to congratulate him on at last putting the truth out there for the Aussie supporters to read. How the hell can it have been the best performance ever when they were playing against 11 men?

One of the things that struck me about playing for Great Britain was it seemed too many players thought it more important to play in a Challenge Cup Final at Wembley than represent the national side. To me I had reached the top of the tree in Rugby League representing my country, and there was no higher honour in my opinion. I was proud to pull on that red, white and blue shirt. I remember later being selected to play for GB away against France and I had to go and get my very first passport. I still have it, together with the stamp the French customs put in it. That is how proud I was to play for Great Britain.

The other thing that was a big shock was that, when the international team got together, they did not have a designated coach who would decide how they were going to play. The team was selected by a board of selectors, and the secretary of the league, Bill Fallowfield, was a sort of team manager and that was it. The players decided amongst themselves how they would play the game, which was crazy to my mind and something I could not understand. The Aussies were much better organised, having been together for a number of weeks, and they also they seemed to have worked out a game plan before the match kicked off. We were simply playing an international match 'off the cuff' which didn't make any sense.

Having been on the wrong end of the thrashing at Swinton in the second Test, I thought that was my international career over and done, but luckily that proved not to be the case. The selectors must have seen something in my performance at Station Road that had impressed them because when the team for the third Test was announced – the selectors making wholesale changes to the side – there were only three players who kept their place: Gower at full back, John Stopford on the wing and me. I was the only forward to keep his shirt and when we played the third Test over at Headingley, the much changed pack was: Collier, Ward, Watson,

Huddart, Roberts and Don Fox. In truth I think they had picked a side that was going to take no prisoners with players who were prepared to dish it out, if that was what was needed to win the game. I remember when we got together, Bill Fallowfield said to us, 'We have never lost a Test match at Leeds and we are not starting now.' That was the attitude we took out on the field with us that afternoon and losing was not an option.

The Aussies were as pumped up as we were as they were wanting a whitewash in the series. They had won the Ashes in England for the first time in ages and were wanting to rub it in. There is no doubt that our pack was short on finesse and class but it was not short on the physical stuff. Right from the start there was a bit of thumping and the referee, Eric Clay, was determined that the game was not going to get out of hand. He sent Barry Muir off early doors for kicking one of our lads. Barry swore blind he had only kicked at the ball. Clay did not see it that way and sent him for an early bath. He was followed by a second Aussie, Brian Hambly, and that really turned the game our way, but we had taken no prisoners right from the kick-off and not once taken a backward step. Toward the end of the first half, as we packed down, one of the Aussie second-rowers gave me a crack on the head, so as I stood up I stuck my knee right in his face. Eric Clay had a field day reading me the riot act and I didn't dare answer him back when he was in that sort of mood. I was left in no doubt that any such further play would see me having an early bath alongside the two Aussies.

We went in for the half time break in front and Bill Fallowfield told us just to keep doing the same, keep the game tight and take no prisoners. As we took the field for the second half, I was stood, as props did back then, out on the touchline and the ten yard line waiting for the kick-off. I remember I was hunched over with my hands on my knees looking down at the ground waiting for the Aussies to come out. As they ran out onto the field, Peter Dimond, the Aussie wingman, gave me a smack across the head as he ran passed me. The game had not even kicked off and I had taken a punch to the head! I thought, right you bugger, I am going to have you and no mistake.

As the second half got started I chased Dimond all over the place but could not get a tackle on him, or even get close to him. Eventually he got the ball and was being tackled by a couple of our lads, I raced across on the wet ground to give them a hand but I lost my footing and, as Dimond hit the ground, I slid into him and hit him with my knees. I thought it was pretty innocent and certainly was not intentional, that was not my style, but the referee did not see it that way as he blew the whistle and pointed straight to the dressing room.

I am not sure if he sent me off in an attempt to even up the game in some way, or if he felt he had to having warned me in the first half. Certainly he had let far worse things go than my knees crashing into Dimond. Luckily the sending off did not affect us as we won the game 16-5 and avoided the whitewash the Aussies desperately wanted. I remember when I went to the disciplinary meeting, in my defence I pleaded it was a case of mistaken identity. Unfortunately they watched the television replay and saw just what had happened. Guilty as charged your honour!

When the Aussies left for home, we had only the French to play. They could be hard and tough opponents in my day, unlike today, but they were not in the same league as the lads from down under. I think that in all the games I played against France, we won just as many as we lost. I am not saying that the French had good players but they sure as hell had bloody good referees!

The French team had several players who were a real nasty piece of work. One of them kicked Tommy Bishop in the nuts and the bruising was so bad that at one time they thought Tommy was going to lose one of his balls! I remember on another occasion that we were playing at Central Park and we had Bill Bryant in the pack, he was taking the ball up on the dugout side of the pitch when one of the French players hit him square on the jaw in the tackle. Bill went up in the air and when he hit the deck awkwardly he broke his leg! I think it must be the only time a blow to the jaw resulted in a broken leg.

> *Big Cliff was a very amiable fellow off the pitch, but on it he was a different man. He was the strongest player I ever played with or against, I mean he used to throw 36 gallon barrels of beer up off the floor onto the wagon. Everyone I think is well aware of how physically powerful he was, but what is not so well known was the mental strength he had. He never lost his cool on the field, even when he was in a scrap. We were due to play France in an international match and Cliff, who suffered greatly from migraines, suffered an attack 10 minutes before we were to kick off. He was as white as a ghost but he went out and played. You could have got that Great Britain shirt off his back but you would have had to shoot him first! That is the sort of mental toughness he had, he was not just physically strong and tough.*
>
> *John Warlow St. Helens*

I learned from those first two games I played against

the Aussies that, if you wanted to beat the them, you needed to play with fire in your belly and have a lot of 'mongrel' in you. They do not like it if you run at them and give it to them. You could not afford to let them run the ball about as they would run you off your feet but they did not like it straight up the middle or the rough stuff. Make no mistake, they could dish it out as well as anyone, but if you kept going at them it tended to rattle them more than it rattled us.

*****

It would be three years before I got the opportunity to play against the enemy from down under again. As the 1965-66 season came round, there was the added incentive of a tour down under to play for, as well as all the domestic games.

I never took it for granted that I would make the tour, I just tried to do what I always did which was to go out and put in the same performance week in and week out. I never liked training but would do it if I felt I needed to. I was very fit, particularly for the era and the position I was playing in, as I was by then working for a brewery – which was a laugh seeing as I did not drink then – and spent all day throwing 36 gallon barrels of beer about. I suppose, in a day, I would probably also throw around two hundred crates full of bottled beer and the same number with empties in them. I certainly didn't need a weights programme as my job took care of that!

In addition to training we were playing twice a week. I used to laugh at Abe Terry and Bob Dagnall when they were training. Up at the back of the pitch we had a little sprint track and Abe and Bob would come in and put on a plastic sweat suit along with a tracksuit and a woolly scarf and go up to the track, supposedly to do sprint training. They always looked very professional as they prepared for training. Mind you they always took a packet of fags and, after a couple of sprints, they would sit down in a dark corner and have a smoke and a chat! As I said, I never liked training but did it because it was necessary to keep my fitness level up.

As that season progressed, I simply kept trying to be consistent every game I played. I never put myself up on a pedestal thinking I was better than any other player, I just tried to play the same way, game after game. I always tried to learn from every prop I ever played against as they all had their own little tricks to try and win the scrums. If a prop did something to me I had not seen before, I would remember it and try to use it myself. My fitness was good from both my job and training but also from the number of games we used to play in the 1960s with the League, Challenge Cup, Lancashire Cup and the BBC Floodlit Trophy. I have to laugh when I hear players today talking about the workload being too heavy! Bloody hell, we had to work a full week, train twice in the week and many times play two games. Now they train full-time and play once a week and they still complain if they play 20-odd games, I regularly played over 40 and sometimes it got up to 50 in a season if we progressed in the cup competitions.

People kept telling me as the season neared its end that I was certain to go on tour, but I would never count my chickens before they hatched. I must have done something right because I eventually got the call that I was in the tour party to go to Australia and New

Zealand. I cannot tell you how proud I felt when I found out. Here I was a lad from the Midlands, and now I was going to travel to the other side of the world to play Rugby League. It was something I had never dreamt would happen to me.

One interesting thing when I got selected for the tour was it was at the expense of the Wigan Prop, Brian McTigue. Brian was coming to the end of his career but it was still a shock when the selectors left him out of the tour party in favour of me, and the press made a big thing of it. In all the games I played against him he never once said a word to me; he hit me once or twice, yes, but speak to me, no! He never meant anything by that, Brian simply got on with the game, went about his work and there was never any of the sledging from him. When we played Wigan after the tour party was announced, at the end of the game he came over to me, shook my hand and simply said, 'Have a good tour lad.' I thought that was a great gesture on his part and was a measure of the sort of man he was.

Once I knew I had been picked to go down under I had to get permission from my employer, like everyone else at the time. I was lucky that I was working for the family firm of Greenall Whitley and I went to see Mr. Greenall. I told him I was off to Australia and he promised me that my job would be waiting for me when I got home. Back then you had to get your National Insurance book from your employer and take it over to the Rugby League headquarters, as while you were away they put your National Insurance stamp on for you. We were told by the Rugby Football League that while on tour our families would get £5 per week and 10 shillings per child, but I was so excited that it all went over my head – I just wanted to get on the airplane and get over there.

When I left I had even forgotten to leave any money for my wife Barbara to live on, or even arrange for the rugby authorities to get the weekly allowance to her, so she had to go and live with her mother until I got back! I actually still have the player contract for that tour and it showed that we were allowed £3 per week subsistence money while we were in Australia, and when we got home after three months away, we all got paid £301 and three shillings. I had to pay £6 for a pair of tour pants and paid for a cardigan, tie and scarf. The Rugby Football League even charged us for the tour photographs taken both here and in Australia!

When I got to Australia I quickly found that the game was very different to back in England. They also played in different weather conditions. We actually flew into Darwin in the Northern Territories at the top end of the country and played the first game there. Luckily I did not play but Jeff Cookson did, the poor bugger. I think he lost two stone during the game and we played at night! It was very hot and humid, conditions that we were not used to back home. We soon found out that those conditions sapped your energy very quickly. When we went out to play a game we had to play the crowd as well, but I was used to that. What I was not used to was having to play the referee and even the linesmen. I always felt the English officials were very fair. Sometimes you would get the odd one who was influenced by the home crowd, but in Australia it quickly became apparent that any 50-50 decision went against us.

One example that sticks in my mind was the one and only time I was called before the judiciary when I was totally innocent of any charge. We were playing Balmain at the Sydney Cricket Ground and it turned out to be one of those afternoons teams sometimes have. Dave Bolton, the former Wigan player who was at scrum-half for Balmain, was prompting and cajoling his team all over the park and he had led his side into a 9-8 lead as the game was coming to its end. In the last few minutes we managed to put it all together and got the ball away to our wingman, Bill Burgess from Barrow. Bill got to the line and grounded the ball but he did not let go of it, he just picked it up again as he was continuing moving. Then his opposite number came in and tackled him into touch at which point the linesman put his flag up and the referee ruled no try!

As you can imagine, Bill Burgess was not best pleased, and he remonstrated with the linesman telling him he had touched down and picked the ball up again from the ground. The linesman would have none of it and the pair of them got into a fair old argument. Tommy Bishop and myself went over and Tommy tried to calm the situation, but neither of them would let it go. I actually thought that Bill and the linesman would come to blows, and so did Tommy, so he stepped between the two of them and pushed them apart. The next thing we know is that the referee and the linesman tell us they are going to cite Tommy for manhandling a match official. You can well imagine the result of that, Bill was as mad as hell, and Tommy was even madder because the touch judge had claimed that he had assaulted him! Tommy even apologised to both the referee and the touch judge but the touchy was having none of it and claimed he was going to report Tommy and Bill to the authorities.

Things looked like they could get totally out of hand

and in the end Bill Fallowfield came down to the pitch side and calmed the two of them down, telling them to leave it until the Tuesday when the judiciary down in Phillips Street would hear the matter.

Tuesday duly arrived and I was called as a witness and I went in and told the board exactly what had happened. They realised that the linesman had made a blunder and they didn't want any bad publicity, so they ruled there was no case to answer and the charge was dismissed. They knew that Bill had scored but the result still stood and it went down as a loss 9-8, but it also highlights the difficulties we faced with Australian officials on that tour.

As we approached that first Test, the Aussie press, in typical manner, had already written us off. We had not started the tour well and had lost four of our first nine games, so the media reckoned that, as their team had won the Ashes over in England, they were going to retain them with ease at home. I was lucky enough to get picked for the first Test and we got, in my opinion, one of the best referees around in Australia at the time in Jack Bradley. He gave us a fair go and not only did we win the Test but I actually scored. I was like a dog with two dicks about that I can tell you. We completely outplayed the Aussies that day and we did not have Harry Poole, our first choice loose forward, playing. I remember the try I got well; the Aussies had not really seen a lot of me and I don't think they realised just how quick I was for a prop. I got a pass and saw a gap, charged through, bumped off a couple of forwards and got the ball over the line. I was proud as punch to score a try against the Aussies in the first Test of the series, and in their own back yard.

The ref in the game did drop the most enormous clanger though. My mate, John Mantle, took a ball up and he had a habit of running across field and suddenly straightening up to go through a gap. I watched him take the ball up and knew exactly what he was going to do, but so too did Langlands the Aussie full back. He tracked John and, as he straightened up, he hit him with a stiff arm right across the chops. Johnny went down like a sack of spuds, he got up, fell down, rolled around, got up then fell down again. Langlands had caught him with a good one and John never really recovered from it during that game. The really daft thing was that Langlands had smacked John and I think all of the players and most of the spectators in the ground had seen it but, when the fight that ensued had settled down and order restored, the ref called over Ken Irvine and gave him a caution for a high tackle. I just fell about laughing. Jack McNamara, who was covering the game for the British newspapers, was up in the press box, miles away from the action, and even he saw it. He wrote: 'Mantle was tackled by Langlands who nearly took his head off his shoulders. Mantle ran to the sideline, collapsed, ran back onto the field and pitch-forked on to his face. When he got up, he spent a long time on one knee trying to get over the tackle.'

As is always the case when the Aussies lose, the authorities seem to want to look for reasons for the defeat from outside the team. They and the press never seemed to be able to admit that the Aussies had been outplayed by a better team on the day. They do not want to be critical of their own players. They do, however, need a scapegoat and the soft target is always the one blowing the whistle. It was the same after that first Test defeat, so the focus was put on Bradley and his performance. Really we had played very well and deserved to win but the Aussie officials and press did not see it that way. None of the Aussie press gave us credit for that win, I think they were smarting and felt that they may well lose the Ashes and needed to do something to prevent that, and do something they did.

I was quite keen after the game to see just what the press had made of the try I scored that had set us on the road to victory. I should have known what was coming but I was a bit miffed when the local reporter, Christensen, wrote of the score: 'Watson ran through the Australian forwards from 20 yards out and, although it appeared as though he had lost the ball in diving for a try, referee Bradley ruled the big cockney had scored.'

It seemed that even the journalists had to find an excuse for the defeat and Christensen had a dig at the referee knowing full well he could not answer back, but it all added to the pressure the Aussie referee was coming under following the defeat.

We went into the second Test knowing that the Aussies would come at us hard, but the officials must have thought that Bradley was perhaps not as harsh on us as he should have been – or put another way, as easy on the home team as he could have been. He was dropped and replaced by Col Pearce who penalised us to death and we lost the game 6-4. There was not a try scored; Keith Barnes knocked over three penalties and we could manage only two. I think we knew that the writing was on the wall from the way the game had been handled as the ref penalised the life out of us. He seemed to blow the whistle whenever we were getting a roll on and even penalised the home team at times to slow us down. Even then we could have actually still won the game. Our wingman, Wrigglesworth, set off across the Aussie line of defence and shot through a gap. Having made the break he drew the defence and threw out a pass to the other wingman, Bill Burgess. Had Burgess caught the ball it was a certain try, but sadly the ball was dropped and with it the game was lost.

Pearce also made sure that our task was not going to be an easy one when he sent Bill Ramsey off for an alleged kick. Our centre, Ian Brooke, was pole-axed by an Aussie who clothes lined him and Bill took exception. Bill had taken a stiff arm in the first half and the referee had done nothing but Bill went in swinging, as was his usual style. From what I saw of the incident someone gave him a push and he fell over and, as he did so, his leg went up in the air but it never connected with anyone. The next thing Pearce is blowing his whistle like a steam train and Bill was given his marching orders. Given the Aussies had won the Ashes over in England in 1963 playing against 11 men, maybe Pearce felt it would be easier if they did the same again.

It was after the second Test that I contracted septicaemia from a cut I got in the game. I did not really clean the wound as well as I should have and paid the price. We had to get the doctor out at about 2.00am a couple of days later as my leg and groin had swollen alarmingly.

The other thing I remember about that game was not only were the players battling, the supporters on the terraces were also giving it some. They had too much ale and, at times, their scrapping actually spilled out onto the field. I thought it was all hilarious. We had to stop playing while the stewards stopped spectators from fighting!

I knew that we were now facing an uphill struggle if we were to take those ashes back home. Sure enough when the third Test came round Pearce was still in charge, and we feared the worst. Consequently we lost the Test, narrowly going down 19-14, and with it the Ashes. Once again we were playing the Aussies and the three officials and we just missed out on the top prize. McNamara, the British press reporter, summed it up in his coverage of the game with the headline: ROBBED OF ASHES BY REF.

The press were not too enamoured with us that day. They referred to the game as a blood bath, and they made a great deal of the fact that the Aussie prop Noel Kelly and I had a few fisticuffs. Certainly Kelly was not going to back down and I was not either, but that was the way Test matches were played then and should be played today. I went out of my way to ensure I ran the ball at Kelly, or was in a position to tackle him when he took the ball up, and he did the same to me. It was a hard, physical contest and there were lots of other such battles throughout the game with other players. Sadly once again I got into a clean bath, and once again it was Peter Dimond who was responsible for me leaving the field early in the second half and us waving the Ashes behind in Australia.

We had gone into that third Test feeling that if the referee gave us a fair go, then we had a great chance of winning the match. Sadly the referee made sure we had no chance. My old mate and arch enemy Dimond had been putting himself about a bit, and Pearce had spoken to him at least three times about his play. Early in the second half, Dimond ran at me and actually dropped on a loose ball just as I was kicking it. He then hit the ground and started to roll over and over in a dying swan act which conned the referee who blew up. The next thing the linesman on the opposite side of the field ran on from 50 yards away waving his flag like a maniac and told the referee that I had kicked Dimond. The result was I took a long walk for an early bath and left my mates to play that last 30-odd minutes on their own.

As I was walking off the field, Dimond was on the ground laughing his head off. A minute or so later he was setting off on a run with the ball. Talk about a quick recovery; his must have been a miracle recovery if I had kicked him as hard as he made out.

We lost the game and with it the Ashes, but on the Tuesday at the Judiciary I gave it to the Aussies big style. I told them straight, 'You have won the bloody Ashes what more do you want? The referee saw nothing and it was the touch judge away on the other side of the pitch that reported me. If I had kicked him with my size 12 boots he would not have got up. As it was not a minute later he ran 60 yards with the ball in his bloody hands!'

The result was no case to answer and the judiciary cleared me but we had once again had to play a good part of the game with a man short, and as a result we went home empty handed. As that game had ended there was a massive blue when one of the Aussies poleaxed Dave Robinson with a high shot. Everyone piled in and fists were flying everywhere. Once again Pearce sat on his whistle. And the odd thing was no Aussies were with me on that Tuesday night at the judiciary to answer for felling Robinson!

I would say at this point that there were a lot of fun times on that tour, particularly when the lads played tricks on each other. Peter 'Flash' Flanagan, the Hull KR hooker, was one who seemed to get a bit of stick. Not long after we arrived in Australia it became known that he and Dave Robinson, who were roomed together, were absolutely terrified of rats, mice, cockroaches and the like. While we were downstairs one evening, one of the lads sneaked into Flash's room and placed a dead rat on his bed. When he went to bed we were all waiting outside the room and heard the scream. Flash threw the rat out of the window. Next morning at breakfast he quipped, 'Bloody touring here is just a rat race,' which cracked us up. On another occasion we were up country and in a hotel where the cockroaches were as big as saucers. Flash and Dave Robinson were late for an early morning training session, so Jack Harding went up to their room. When he went in and called out, two heads popped up from under their sheets. The poor buggers were so scared of the big cockroaches they had taken cover in their beds!

On that tour it was the first and only time I missed a game because of sunburn. We were up in Queensland and on a day off had sailed over to Green Island on the Great Barrier Reef. When we got there, we all took our shirts off and an old Aussie told us to be careful as the sun was particularly fierce. After half an hour or so we all covered up, but on the sail back the weather changed and it became overcast, so Johnny Mantle, Colin Clarke and myself were up at the front of the boat in just our swimming costumes getting splashed by the water coming over the bow. We did not think there would be a problem as the cloud was blocking out the sun – or so we thought. Boy did we pay for it the next day. The three of us were covered in blisters and unfit to play.

The managers were not amused I can tell you and gave us a right good bollocking.

The game today lacks the intensity that Test matches had back when I played. A lot of that is due to the television and the softening of the physical side of the game. When I played, there was a great deal of physical stuff that went unseen. Often the referees may have missed an offence but they knew they had and would give you a warning on the run. They would say something to the effect of, 'I know something went on back there and I missed it but I have got my eye on you mate!' Certainly I think that Test matches between Great Britain and Australia were always blood and guts affairs, very physical with no quarter asked or given. The nearest thing today is the Origin series in Australia. However, it brasses me off when I hear people telling us that State of Origin is the peak of any player's career! What a load of crap; the pinnacle is pulling on your country's colours. For sure, in that deciding third Test match we didn't get a fair crack of the whip from Col Pearce, in fact it would be true to say we never even saw the bloody whip!

On that 1966 tour, I am convinced we could have won the series but we contributed to our own downfall which was annoying. We were very well led by Brian Edgar, the other prop. Brian was a great ball-handling forward who could put players through gaps but he had to work on his own. And yet we had another superb ball handler in Harry Poole sitting on the touchline twiddling his thumbs, and he was the tour captain. The reason for that was all down to our own bloody physiotherapist, Paddy Armour. He was forever away giving lectures or demonstrations at Rugby League clubs and you could never get a rub down from him, that was for sure. It was all you could do to get him to strap you. Harry Poole had a problem with his knee, which would always swell up after training. He had learned to live with it and with the pain. He regularly played with the knee strapped, but after training when we were on tour, Paddy would keep telling the management that he was not fit, that the knee would break down and he would not last the game out. The result was that Harry, instead of being on the field, was sat on his arse warming a seat in the stands. There was no one more annoyed than Harry but the management would not overrule the physio, despite all that Harry said.

To give you an example of what I mean when I say we greatly missed Harry, we played a Sydney City side and they actually selected a strong team – I think to soften us up for the upcoming Test. Harry was selected to play and during the game we did not get a fair go from the referee. In the end Tommy Bishop got upset and started putting himself about a bit and that fired us up. Harry, as skipper, decided he was going to join in the mayhem Tommy was creating. At the time we were losing the game 14-2. Harry, just out on the fringes, began knocking Sydney players about in defence and spraying the ball about like only he could when we were on the attack. I remember Kevin Ryan was playing for Sydney and he was a hard man, but Harry gave him better than he got that second half. Johnny Mantle and I had a field day running onto the passes Harry kept putting out and we shocked the press and the opposition when we turned the game around and won 15-14.

I would not want to be disrespectful to Dave Robinson the other loose forward on the tour, who was a great player, but he was a player in a different mould to Harry. Dave was like a machine and you could never tire the bugger out. I remember on one occasion the selectors on tour, realising he had played 14 games on the trot, decided to rest him and so did not pick him for a game. Dave got very upset thinking he had been dropped when in fact they were giving him a rest!

There is no doubt in my mind that if Harry had played in the Test matches we would have won the series. We would have had a ball handler out on the fringes in Harry and a ball handler down the middle with Brian Edgar. Brian was feared by the Aussies, not only for his ball handling, but he could look after himself in the rough stuff as well. Brian could thump alongside the best of them and the Aussies knew it. Mind you, Harry was no slouch in that department either come to think of it. But further out on the fringes the gaps were a little wider, and Harry would have torn the Aussie defence apart had he been allowed to play. We should have had Harry in the team for the second and third Tests. It was bad enough losing the Ashes but to think we had contributed to our own downfall pissed me off I can tell you.

The following year when the Aussies came over to England we also lost the series two to one, and once again the referee played a big part in our downfall. Unfortunately this time it was one of our own whistle blowers. As the second Test was to be played down in London, the Rugby Football League decided to push the boat out and organised us a stay in the capital. We were in camp prior to that second Test in 1967 down in London and both the Aussies and the Great Britain players were billeted at the same place – I think it was at The White City. It was quite funny at breakfast time as the Aussies would be at one end of the dining room and we would be up at the other and neither side spoke to each other. We always thought that the ref, Fred Lindop, who was also with us and had been named to referee the three Test games got a bit too friendly with the opposition during that stay, so much so that the GB players renamed him Aussie Lindy.

We had gone to Headingley for the first Test and, true to form, had turned the Aussies over winning 16-11. I think it was the eighth or ninth Test against the Aussies we had won on the trot at Leeds. We had been under the cosh for the first 15 minutes or so and the Aussies could have scored a couple of tries, but we held out and gradually turned the game around. My mate, John Mantle, had a great game that afternoon and was instrumental in setting up Roger Millward to score the try for us that put us back in front. Although the score was close we were always in control in that game once we settled down.

The second Test was a different story as the game was to be played under the floodlights at The White City stadium. There was a big crowd and most of them were Aussies staying and working in London. The Aussies won that game 17-11 to square the series. As always seemed to be the case when I was playing against the Aussies, we went into the final Test match with the Ashes at stake. The game was due to be played at Station Road in Swinton on December 9th and when match day rolled round we were all in for a shock.

On the Saturday the snow had been falling and the pitch was white over. The weather had been icy in the run up to the weekend and, as was always the case back then, straw had been placed over the turf in an attempt to stop the ground from freezing, but it was not very successful. When we arrived at the ground, the place was swarming with folk shifting straw and sweeping the snow off the lines so that the game could go ahead. The fact was the ground was unfit to play on but the Rugby Football League and the match officials decided that the game should go ahead. I am not sure if the officials had been pressurised by the RFL to do so but the game, had it been cancelled, would not have been replayed and the series tied and the Ashes undecided. The reason for that was that the Aussies were to fly over to France the following day and once they finished there they were to go home. We did not really want to play but the Aussies did and the hard freezing ground suited them more than us as, apart from the difference in temperature, the hard ground was just like playing down in Sydney. In the end we lost the game and with it the series.

Once the game started a blizzard swept across the ground and did not let up the whole 80 minutes. The driving sleet and snow made even seeing hard and the ball difficult to handle. It was a tough, hard encounter and in my opinion Lindop did us no favours during the game. With the scores very close the Aussies were on the attack and Ron Coote went in for what turned out in the end to be the winning score. In truth I was quite close to the incident, covering across the pitch, and Coote was at least two feet short of the line when he was actually tackled. The ref was a fair way off, looking through a blizzard, but he pointed to the spot and awarded the try.

We walked off the field at the end 3-11 down, and for the third time I was on the losing end of an Ashes series and was pretty sick about it. We had lost in Australia thanks to dodgy refereeing and had suffered the same fate at home. It was hard to take. Two Test series' we should really have won had been lost and the Aussies were crowing about it.

*****

Early in the 1968-69 season, I was honoured to be selected to captain England in a game against Wales. It was the first time in 15 years that the two countries had met and, on Thursday November 7th, 1968, the lad from Dudley ran out at the Willows to lead his country. Believe me there is no greater feeling than that. I was as proud as punch to have that honour, but the downside was that we lost the game.

I remember it as if it were yesterday. Billy Thompson refereed the game and there were 6,000 in the ground that night. Mind you all did not go according to plan because on the morning of the game, Alex Murphy, who had been selected to play for England, pulled out. The Rugby Football League had to get on the phone and try to locate Tommy Bishop to come in and replace him. At the time Tommy was working for the Gas Board in St. Helens and, as this was pre-mobile phones, the Gas Board were unable to contact Tommy. A call went out to the Leeds player, Mick Shoebottom, and he came into the side. After about 20 minutes of the game, Shoebottom got injured and had to come off, so we finished the game with Davis at scrum-half and Chris Hesketh playing stand-off while Alan Buckley came into the centre. I found it a bit strange as there were so many Saints players in the Welsh side and John Mantle was actually captaining them. In the pack there were

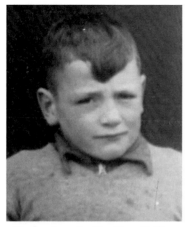

Early days in Dudley. Still a bit of growing to do

Dib dib dib, the height of things to come

An improvised weight training session at Newey Brothers

Early days with Dudley Kingswinford. I am third from the left on the back row

Barbara and I tie the knot

A very proud Saint

The 1961 Challenge Cup Final and there is no way Terry Entwistle is getting the ball

Back at Wembley in 1966 and I get to say hello to Prime Minister Harold Wilson

Chasing Billy Boston down at Wembley was becoming a habit!

Does it suit me? I was just as proud winning the Challenge Cup in 1966 as I had been the first time

The Chamionship Trophy and a good job well done

I did a different sort of weight training when I joined Saints

My brother and I celebrate my first cap

A typical charge – head-down, arse-up – against the old enemy

Big Artie Beetson and I get to it

Another example of how to take the ball up

The best feeling in the world, scoring a try at the Sydney Cricket Ground against Australia

I was very proud to hold aloft the Ashes Trophy after we won it in the Aussies' backyard

The Ashes come back home for the last time

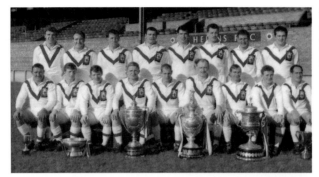

Saints' five cups-
winning season.
I'm on the back row
fourth from the left

I told you Frenchy that
blow golf would never
catch on!

One happy skipper
holding the trophy

I could not get my bloody
finger out of the handle and
thought I would have to take
the cup home with me

A broken arm cost me a place in the Final but I did get a cap

An early introduction to my new team-mates at Cronulla

Who said I was not a ball playing prop forward?

Tommy Bishop and I discuss tactics before the Grand Final

Cronulla Sharks in the lead up to the Grand Final. I am third from
the left on the back row

Centre stage, same colours as Saints but it is the Wollongong Hawks

I was honoured to be selected in the Greatest 17 St. Helens Players in 2010.
I am third from the left on the front row

four Saints forwards and it was a little difficult playing against them. I had trained with them at Saints on the Tuesday and had to play against them two days later. I do remember getting into a set-to with John Warlow at one time, but that was John, you could be his best mate but on the field you simply became the opposition and he treated everyone the same.

What I found amazing was that we all simply turned up at Salford and played, there was no coach designated to look after the England team. I cannot even remember if we actually had a manager for the side. That tells you just how far back we were from the Aussies even then. The Welsh scored five tries to our four and were more successful with their goal kicking too and we lost 24-17. I was pleased to have captained England that night and would have loved to have been captain of a Great Britain side, but sadly that never happened, it is the one honour I never got from the game.

I have played in Test matches against New Zealand and France, and had a lot of success, but it was never the same as playing against the green and gold of Australia. In those games the intensity was ramped up a lot higher. In 1968 I was back down under with Great Britain, this time in the World Cup, and we did not do ourselves justice. There were quite a number of Leeds players in that World Cup squad and I just felt we never really blended into a team that was capable of winning the cup. It was not something I could really put my finger on. It was not really a clique thing but the whole team never seemed to gel into a cohesive unit capable of winning the trophy. I think we had too many show ponies and not enough workhorses; by show ponies I mean players who liked to run on top of the ground and do the fancy stuff and we paid the price. We played Australia at the Sydney Cricket Ground and lost 25-10 and so we were on the back foot from then on.

When we went over to New Zealand to play France, we got our team selection wrong on the day. We were to play them at Carlaw Park and the pitch was a quagmire due to all the rain we had had for a couple of days prior to the game. But we picked players who liked to run on the top of the ground, which was impossible on the day. We needed 'mud runners'; players who would get the ball and run head-down, arse-up at the French rather than trying to move the ball about as we tried to do. That is what the French did to us all afternoon, simple straight up and down the field rugby, and they walked out of Carlaw Park winners by 7-2. We kept trying to play rugby but the pitch would not let us and the French handled all we could throw at them. We beat New Zealand in our next game but, because of the loss to France, we did not make the Final, and in the end the Aussies won the World Cup quite easily.

With our competition over, we were all ready to get on a plane and come home, but it was not to be. The tour manager, Bill Fallowfield, got a visit from a football manager from Mount Isa up in the north of Queensland, a big mining area. He suggested to Bill that if the team were to travel up and play against a Mount Isa district team then he could make it worthwhile. Bill put it to us all and we decided to go. We were in the dressing room up there trying to put a team together; Ray French had bad blisters and was hobbling a bit, John Warlow was nursing a number of damaged fingers and we were a bit like the walking wounded. It was then that the guy from Mount Isa came in to the dressing room to ask about how many substitutions he was allowed to use. Bill Fallowfield told him two as that was the International Board rules. The manager's face fell and he scratched his head. He proceeded to tell Bill he had 26 players who wanted to play against us! It was finally agreed that we would let him feed on subs as he liked and we went out to play the game.

We won the game against Mount Isa easily, 33-5, but when they actually managed to score their try, all 26 of their players did a lap of honour they were so pleased. The gate was only around 2,300 but they were all paying $40 to get in, and being miners they had money to burn, so we got a good pay packet out of the trip. Even with that game over we still could not get home. We were due to fly with British Airways but their pilots went on strike, so Quantas offered to fly us to Darwin or Hong Kong where we could stay until the strike was over. Well you would not want to spend four or five days in Darwin, that's for sure, so the team finished up in Hong Kong. While I was there I went to get a suit made and the tailor wanted to charge me £20. The pilot from Quantas who had flown us in was with me and his name was Henry Chan. He negotiated with the tailor and I paid a tenner in the end, and three hours later I went and picked up a brand new suit.

I remember that competition in the 1968 World Cup. The team never really performed. I think Bev Risman of Leeds was the captain, and we picked footballers rather than all-weather players, particularly against the French. Cliff and I sat on the bench and watched as our lads tried to run the ball about when the mud was coming over the top of their boots – stupid. In the 1970 World Cup we got to the Final and played in the so called battle of Headingley. Cliff was like a madman; he was all over the pitch tackling and running the ball up. He was a fierce tackler but he was not one for thumping you in the tackle – he had no need to, he hit you so bloody hard as it was. He just desperately wanted to beat the Aussies every time he went onto the pitch.

John Warlow, St. Helens

By this time I was beginning to get a bit frustrated about the Aussie situation as they seemed to constantly be a monkey on our backs. I had to wait until 1970 to do something about it. I played in the 1970 World Cup and I really thought that we would win that competition as we had got through to the Final without losing a game.

We had beaten the Aussies and followed it up with wins over New Zealand and France. Everyone felt we would beat the Aussies once more in the Final. Sadly it turned out not to be the case as the game at Headingley turned into a running battle from start to finish. We won a mountain of possession and could not use it. We did not seem to be able to play any decent football at all. I know that John Ledger, writing in the *Yorkshire Post*, felt it was one of the dirtiest, most ill-tempered Test matches of all time. I also know that referee Lindop blew for time a minute or so after sending off Syd Hynes and Billy Smith. It was after he blew time that it all kicked off and there was a mass brawl. The only player not involved was the Aussie centre, John Cootes, the Catholic priest. Mind you, him being a priest had not stopped me earlier in the game from giving him a smack! We walked off the field losers once again by a score of 12-7, and that monkey was not only sitting on my back but was bloody laughing at me as well.

As the 1969-70 season was coming to an end, there was another tour down under in the offing, and this time I really was hoping to get the call up. I did what I always did which was to try to be as consistent as I could in my game. I think I was helped in that by being the captain at Saints that season. I thrived on the extra responsibility of being captain and tried to lead from the front every week. The selectors must have thought that I could still do a job as they selected me for the squad. In many respects, going on that second tour was a little like when I went to Wembley for the second time. I was more experienced and more aware of the game in Australia than I was the first time, and I was also more successful second time round. Frank Myler was to captain the touring side and, to my great delight, I was appointed vice-captain – you have no idea how that made me feel. I had been proud to captain St. Helens and I was over the moon now to have a similar role with Great Britain!

The coach on that tour in 1970 was John Whiteley, the former Hull player, and he proved to be a superb coach on and off the field in Australia. He had toured as a player himself and so was able to see things from our point of view. When we got down under, he told all of the players in a meeting early on that, while he was in charge, there would be no 'ham and eggers'. On previous tours, the players were tending to be looked on as either Test match players, who performed on the weekend, or non-Test match players who played in mid-week. The mid-week players were always called the 'ham and eggers' and it could and did lead to a two-team mentality creeping in. Whiteley was having none of that in his party, everyone was a potential Test player and he told us so. The players responded accordingly and they would have done anything for him. I have to say that the tour manager, Jack Harding, was equally as good. He was a decent, down-to-earth man and would help any player, whatever their standing in the game. It didn't matter if you were the most inexperienced tourist or a seasoned veteran, he would move heaven and earth to help you. I think he and Johnny were responsible for all the success the players enjoyed on the tour. Most certainly they both sang from the same hymn sheet throughout the whole tour and the players gave them everything they had.

We set out at the beginning of the tour the way we meant to carry on. We knew we would get no help from the match officials, and we accepted that we would need to get used to the rock hard pitches and the way the players in Australia liked to throw the ball about. We were determined that we would never take a backward step in every game we played and it all worked brilliantly, so much so that we went into the first Test at Lang Park up in Brisbane unbeaten. It was then that things went a little awry for me.

It was a Test match the Aussies remember for all the wrong reasons, but one that started well for me as I managed to cross the line for a try. But in typical fashion in the Test matches, there was a good deal of niggling, punching and a series of fights, right from the kick off. You get some idea of what I mean from what the local reporter up in Brisbane wrote of the game:

> *Within 10 minutes, Australian second-rower, Ron Lynch, was out of the game with a fractured cheekbone. Artie Beetson was bleeding from the mouth and nose and Jim Morgan's nose had been flattened by a quaintly named, but lethal, Liverpool kiss.*

Unfortunately the person responsible for administering the Liverpool kiss to Morgan's nose was yours truly, and it resulted in me being sent off for an early bath. There was a flare-up – one of many – and a load of players were getting involved. Jim Morgan and I had a bit of a square up of our own in the midst of all this that got a bit out of hand. I had hold of Morgan's shirt and was trying to stop him punching me. This resulted in Jim trying to head-butt me. He had a couple of goes at me and caught me on the side of the head, but did not get it right, so I decided to show him how it should be done. I caught him just right and it flattened his nose – there was blood and snot everywhere. Jim actually stayed on the field and carried on playing, going on to score two tries as the Aussies won the first Test by 37-15. Whereas I got an early bath and the rabid press hounding after me.

In typical Aussie fashion, the press went totally overboard. They were writing about a vicious attack and were proposing that I should be banned for life. There was even a move in the press to ban me from ever playing the game again on Aussie soil. When you think of the mayhem that was going on week in, week out in the Aussie domestic game at that time, their attitude toward me was ridiculous. Brawls and players punching each other were everyday occurrences in Aussie Rugby League at the time and the press did not seem to mind, but when the tourists started to do it the shit really hit the fan. I really could not understand what all the fuss was about; I had been sent off and would get suspended, serve it and get back to playing, end of story.

To his great credit, Jim Morgan was totally honest in the dressing room after the match when interviewed by the press. They tried to get him to have a go at me for the head-butt, however, he told them straight that it was he who had tried to head-butt me first, and that he had got it wrong and I had got it right. I respected him greatly for that because he could have rubbished me and added more fuel to the fire the press were already lighting under me.

When I eventually moved down under I became good mates with Jim, and often my wife and I would go out to dinner with him and his wife. I would say, however, that the incident ruined his career. In the third Test when we scrummed down for the first time, we greeted him with the words, 'How's your nose Jim?' When we did, there was no reply from Jim, nothing came back at us from him. If someone had said that to me, I would have given them a smack there and then, but I think Jim only played one more game for Australia after that third Test. The incident, which brought me a great deal of notoriety in a funny sort of way, did the same for Jim, but we did remain the best of mates until the day he died of a heart attack while he was swimming in the surf.

Cliff was and is a great friend of mine and I am proud of what he achieved in the game, and what he achieved on that 1970 tour. That front row of Dennis Hartley, Tony Fisher and Cliff Watson was the last time Great Britain, in my opinion, had an international front row. You have to remember on that tour we had a lot of young players who were, perhaps, a little underweight as well as inexperienced. Cliff stood up and said, 'I will lead these lads and lead from the front,' and boy he did just that. In that first Test in Brisbane the claret was flowing, but players like Jim Thompson and Mal Reilly, along with Cliff, showed real English guts, muscle and brains, and in Tests it all stems from your front row, and we had a good one. *If your front three are doing their job, it becomes easy for the rest to do theirs.*

I know the Aussie press had written us off after that first Test but we hadn't. What people forget is that we started that tour the wrong way round. Generally you start down in Sydney and play five or six of the Sydney sides, then by the time the first Test comes along you are battle hardened. For some reason we started up in the Northern Territories and North Queensland, and the teams we played were really fodder to our lads. When we got to Sydney we were not that battle hardened and the Aussies literally blew us away.

After that first Test defeat I let the lads go on the piss over the weekend, but on Monday morning we all sat down and discussed what we were going to do. Both Cliff and Mal said they were going to roll their sleeves up and give the Aussies as good as they gave us. I think Cliff getting sent off, and the manner of it, gave us a great deal of resilience, and that resilience was strengthened at that Monday meeting. We resolved never to back away from anything and to make sure the Aussies knew it. We went on from that meeting to win the Ashes back.

As a player I was fortunate enough to play with and against Brian McTigue, the great Wigan prop, and I will say this, that as Great Britain coach, if I had had Brian and Cliff in their prime in my team, I would not have needed the other four forwards to beat the Aussies. That is how good I think they were.

Cliff came into the game from a Rugby Union background but he was as tough as teak, and on the tour he relished the role of mentor to the younger players and they looked up to him for guidance, on and off the field. He had no favourites and treated everyone the same and he had a lovely heart. He was never going to back down from any challenge and I think he knew full well what he could

aspire to in the game and worked hard to get there.
For me on that tour, Cliff was a figurehead, and all the players looked up to him and respected him.

Johnny Whiteley, Great Britain coach 1970 tour

All of the lads were pretty down after the defeat in the Test, none more so than me having got sent off. We were not used to losing and had fully expected to win the game. Also we knew that we would be up against it even more now as the referees and touch judges never did give us an even break. We dug deep and Johnny Whiteley and Jack Harding worked hard to revitalise our spirits. We knew we had the beating of the Aussies if we stayed together and kept on doing what we had been doing since the tour started. As a squad we all buckled down and vowed we were not going to take a backward step in any match.

As we prepared for the second Test, we were aware that the whole tour was on the line. A defeat and the Ashes were gone and the tour over as a spectator attraction. As we ran out onto the Sydney Cricket Ground, we all knew just what was at stake, and we delivered a great performance.

Little Roger Millward was in great form and scored two tries as well as kicking six goals. And to add to the Aussie misery, he also banged over a drop goal. The Leeds wingman, John Atkinson, also scored and the hooker, Fisher, crossed the line as well. Syd Hynes put the icing on the cake when he dropped a goal and we walked off after the 80 minutes winners by 28-7. We all felt that we had redeemed ourselves after that first Test loss. What bothered me greatly was that I had been in this situation – one all with one Test to play – a number of times before and come away a loser. It would be a big ask to win the Ashes in Australia, but two weeks later we went out to try to do so.

On July 4th we were again back at the Sydney Cricket Ground for the third and final Test. It was one of those games that either side could have won as the score was so close at the end. But in truth we totally outplayed the Aussies that afternoon, scoring five tries, while they only managed one. The only thing that kept them in the hunt was the penalty goals they kicked. That afternoon we showed the Aussies how the game should be played, and they could not live with us. In the end though, it came down to one bit of magic from Millward, who scored the winning try as we edged out the home side 21-17.

Early in the game, Dennis Hartley charged down a kick and grounded the ball for our first try. Then 10 minutes later, the Aussies were trying to get out of their 25 yard area and Artie Beetson threw out an over the top pass which John Atkinson intercepted to go in for the second. Shortly after, Syd Hynes gathered a kick and scored a third and we went in at half time 15-10 up – the Aussie scores coming from penalties.

In the second half we carried on where we left off and, about 10 minutes in, Mick Shoebottom, who was close to the Aussie line, threw a dummy and then an inside pass to put Atkinson in for his second try. Then with about 20 minutes remaining, I took a ball and drove it up to the 25 yard line when Beetson came in as second man in the tackle and smacked me right on the head with a haymaker. In truth I had been getting up his nose all the game and the fact that we were winning, and winning easily at the time, must have got to Big Artie and so he let one go at me. There was no one more surprised than me at Artie's action as it was completely out of character for him. Although I do reckon that if you get into the faces of the Aussies, and they are behind, they tend to lose it a bit and start swinging instead of playing rugby and perhaps that's what happened with Artie. I always remember him as a brilliant footballer – hard and tough – but not one to be letting punches go. As I said, it was completely out of character.

The Aussie ref, Don Lancashire, had the courage to send Artie off, much to the crowd's annoyance, and no doubt the Aussie rugby officials were not best pleased either. I personally thought the ref was a bit hard on him as there was no way he deserved to be marched. I was okay and ready to carry on playing, and worse things had gone unpunished or simply penalised. However, the ref saw things differently and so we were playing only 12 Aussies when so often it seemed it was the other way round.

The Aussies dug deep and scored a try in the corner to take the score to 18-17. That score drove them on to even greater efforts in an attempt to retain the Ashes while we were also trying to get a score to win them back. In the last minutes of the game, Doug Laughton took the ball up to the line, dropped his shoulder, got through the defensive line and at once slipped out a short pass to Millward who ran 30 yards, rounded the full back and scored the try that gave us the Ashes for sure.

I had been selected for the tour in 1970, but then made the worst decision of my career when I let Roy Francis persuade me to sign for North Sydney and I withdrew from the tour. I went to watch all the Test games and was up in Brisbane when Cliff and Jim Morgan had their set-

to. I think that incident was instrumental in us winning the Ashes because, what Cliff did that day, was to show the Aussie forwards that there would be no backing down by the tourists – if you wanted it rough, boy you were going to get it rough. I was at the third Test when we actually won back the Ashes and I can tell you at the final whistle I have never felt so lonely in my life. It was an unbelievable feeling I had that day. I watched the boys on the field carry that trophy round and felt I could have been on that field with them. Mind you, that day the front row of Cliff, Fisher and Hartley were brilliant.

Jim Mills, Widnes

It was a great feeling, at last I had won an Ashes series against the old enemy and had done so in their own backyard. I took that bloody monkey, which was not laughing any more, wrung its bloody neck and threw it away.

After Australia we went over to New Zealand to play them in three Tests. The first was on July 11th at Carlaw Park on a pitch that looked like a cattle field it was so deep in mud. After battling with the Aussies, it was a bit easier against the Kiwis. We scored another five tries that day – I put Laughton in for the second after charging through a gap. We won the game 19-15, which didn't justify our performance as we dominated them throughout the game.

A week later we went down to Christchurch for the second Test. We weren't at our best in the first half, but we came out for the second 40 minutes fired up and determined to put things right. In the end we were still way ahead of the Kiwis, and we scored another five tries to New Zealand's one to take the win 23-9.

In the final Test back at Carlaw Park on July 25th,

the Kiwis came out fired up for revenge and determined to give it to us. In the first half they played a physical game and went in at the break 11-2 up. They came out for the second half and started targeting Millward with the rough stuff as they reckoned he was a major threat. All that did was wind us up and make us even more determined to knock the shit out of them. We then went on a scoring run, with first Phil Lowe putting the ball down over the line, then I carried three Kiwis over to get our second try. After that the floodgates opened and we ended the game with seven tries, hammering the Kiwis 33-16.

We had won both Test series' and I am sure that no other touring side from England went through a whole Australia and New Zealand tour suffering just one defeat. A lot of the credit for that must go to the players, but also to Johnny Whiteley and his no 'ham and eggers' policy. He ensured that every player felt part of the success and that each felt they were part of the Test team.

No one felt the benefit of Whiteley's attitude more on that tour than the prop Dennis Hartley, the Castleford lad. He had been selected for the tour as a replacement. The Wigan prop, John Stephens, had originally been selected but had dislocated his hip a week or so before we left and Dennis was drafted in. Everyone saw him as being third in line behind myself and Dave Chisnall, but to his credit he never let it bother him. Dennis just knuckled down and worked hard. Whiteley knew Hartley was not fit enough for the game as it was played in Australia and set about putting that right. At the Sydney Sports Ground there is a hill at the side of one of the pitches and, when we had all finished training, Johnny would take Dennis and me out and have us running up and down that hill to get some weight off him and also get him fitter. We called that bloody thing 'Pork Chop Hill'. After that first Test loss, which Dennis did not play in, he was brought in and played the last two Tests and played a great part in us winning the Ashes. It was those sorts of things that the coach did that made it such a great tour.

I remember on one occasion that Mal Reilly had got himself involved in a bit of bother, as only he could. It seems that he had been in a bar and ended up head-butting someone. John Whiteley, Frank Myler and myself went down to the police station and bailed him out. The management wanted to send him home but the three of us said he was too valuable to the team to do that. We had to find money to pay for a lawyer and, as we had a tour 'slush fund', it was agreed we would use that to get him out of trouble. Mal was a difficult player to read at times and could be quite moody. That said I would always have him in my team, but he was a lot like John Sattler, the Aussie prop, in that he could be distant at times. He also reminded me a lot of Vinnie Karalius when his eyes glazed over and he went into the zone before kick off. He seemed to go into himself and was so focussed that you could not get through to him. He was a lot like me though – put a green and gold shirt in front of him, light the blue touch paper and stand by for the firework display that was inevitably going to follow.

Again it was not all serious stuff on that tour, there were funny and odd moments as well. Hartley and a couple of us went out one day to a beauty parlour to get a massage. After the massage we got a haircut and the hairdresser told Dennis that he should get a toupee as it would take years off him. We talked him into agreeing and the guy fitted the toupee and it really did knock 10 years off him. When we went to the hotel for dinner, no one noticed the piece and Dennis was as happy as Larry. Early the next morning I got a phone call in my room. It was Dennis panicking that he could not refit the toupee and could I help him. Well we tried and tried but could not get it right so we put it in a paper bag, took it back and got our money back.

On another occasion we were playing up country and came face to face once again with the stupidity of some Aussie referees. The curtain raiser before we played was a game involving two Aborigine teams. They were playing the game barefoot and kicking the ball with no trouble. When we went out to play, after a time Frank Myler got the most enormous blisters so decided that he would take his boots off. The ref told him to put his boots back on. Frank said the players in the warm up game had been playing barefoot so what was the difference. The ref told him he was playing first grade football and if he did not put his boots on he would send him off the field! Frank was fuming but had to put the boots back on to carry on playing the game.

Little did I know back then, as I held that Ashes trophy aloft at the Sydney Cricket Ground, that it would be the last time England would win an Ashes series; a fact that saddens me greatly. If I was going to draw the curtain down on my international playing career, then there was no finer way to bow out than after winning the Ashes, and winning them back down under. However, fate had one last little international trick to play on me before my playing career came to an end.

4

A Shark

When I came back from the tour in 1970 it was to my benefit season with St. Helens, having been with the club for ten seasons. I must say that when it came to the organisation of my benefit year, the club were not the greatest help to me and that upset me a little. In truth they did very little at all to help me with the testimonial. In the end I think Ray French and myself organised the whole bloody year, every event. The club said that whatever I raised they would match but in the end they never did. At the end of the season I'd raised £2,000 and the club chipped in not two but one grand to take the total up to £3,000. I was more than a little disappointed with the club's attitude and I felt I deserved better after giving them loyal service for a decade.

Whilst all of this fundraising was going on, I think on the back of my performances on the 1970 tour, a number of Aussie clubs had become interested in getting me out to play in the Sydney competition. At the time Merv Hicks, a former team-mate of mine at Saints, was at Canterbury-Bankstown. I think he was player/coach at the club then and the club actually made contact with me when I was back in England. I got a phone call from them asking me if I was interested in playing in Australia for them. I think they felt that having Merv as their coach would go some way towards swaying me to join them. I told them I would be interested but it would depend on two things, one was the money and the other was that the news that we were in discussions about a move down under must not leak out. I let them know I was in the middle of my benefit season and didn't want to upset the fans, which would be the case if word got out that I was looking to move to an Aussie club. Canterbury understood that I needed the support of the fans to attend the functions Ray and I had organised for my benefit and they kept silent about our dealings.

After talking details with Canterbury I asked them to send over a contract for me to look at and that presented an unusual problem for the club. At the time there was an international postal strike and there was no way they could post a contract off to me. In the end they actually made contact with the Rugby League reporter at the *Yorkshire Post* to act on their behalf. Then they gave the contract to an airline pilot, who was a big Canterbury fan, to take to England on his next trip over. That he did and the reporter collected the contract from him at Manchester Airport. He then brought the contract to me in St. Helens. You get some idea of the way the Rugby League press men operated back then in England as he could very well have written a great story there and then and ruined my benefit season but he did not. We agreed that he would sit on the story and I would inform him should I actually sign the contract so he would get an exclusive. To his credit he kept his side of the bargain and nothing got into the press. I for my part had every intention of keeping my side of the bargain.

I thought I was home and dry and on my way to Canterbury-Bankstown after getting the contract I wanted from them, but somehow, and I even to this day I do not know how, the fledgling Cronulla Sharks club found out that Canterbury were talking to me. Yet another former team-mate of mine, Tommy Bishop, was player/coach at the Sharks and, once he found out I was thinking of coming out to Sydney, he pressed the board into making contact with me. If I was to speculate as to how Tommy found out I would say that perhaps he and Merv Hicks had been talking and Merv let it slip. After all, they had both been team-mates of mine at Saints.

The Cronulla coach, Ken Kearney, had left the club in the 1970 season, and Tommy had been asked to take over as player/coach which he agreed to do. Tommy knew he had a young side and was aware that he needed a pack leader so, once he found out about Canterbury approaching me, he was on the phone like a shot.

Tommy himself rang me and asked if I would be interested in signing for the club, so I told him the same story that I had told Canterbury that they must keep everything under wraps until after my benefit season. Tommy kept ringing and ringing until one day he rang up and I shouted to the missus, 'Tell him I am not in!' I was so sick of talking to the bugger. But that was Tommy, once he got an idea in his head he was like a dog with a bone, he would not let go. Again it was the competitive nature of him that drove him on. He had to win and was determined that he would get me over Canterbury. What I reckoned was that, with two clubs now wanting me, I could play one off against the other, or so I thought.

The next thing I knew was that Arthur Winn and Bob Abbott, senior officials from the Sharks, had hopped on a plane and flown over for a meeting with Basil Lowe and Harry Cook at Saints. I got a phone call in the middle of the afternoon one day asking me if I could go down to the club for a meeting. At the time I was running a scrapyard for Harry Dunn in St. Helens, so I told them straight that I could not just stop working because they wanted a chat with me. Eventually we did meet and it was then that Saints once more upset me. They told me that they were happy to let me go to Sydney but had told the Sharks that they wanted a £12,000 transfer fee. I was not best pleased I can tell you, and let the club know in no uncertain terms. They had paid £1,500 to get me and I had played for nearly 11 season at around £150 a year and they wanted to put a transfer fee on me so high, it was ridiculous.

I told them that Mal Reilly had only cost Manly £15,000 and he was 23 years old whereas I was 30 and they wanted £12,000. They were adamant that they wanted the money or there would be no transfer, so I decided I was going to move down under come what may, even if I was not going to be able to play. I think up to that point I had not really been over bothered about moving over to Australia, but the board's action made my mind up. I felt sorry for the Saints fans who had supported me all through my career and also during my benefit year but I felt hard done to by the Saints board. That day I lost the enthusiasm I'd always had for playing the game for the club as a result of the board's action and decided it was time to move on.

Having made the decision to move, I was in the lucky position of having two clubs that wanted me. I kept talking to both clubs and, in the end, Cronulla came up with the deal I wanted and so I signed for them. When I did sign it was the same time as I broke my arm for the second time, this time against Leeds in the Championship semifinal at the season's end. It was ironic that when I first made contact with St. Helens, way back in 1960, I was nursing a broken arm, and 11 years later as I left the club, I was once again nursing a broken arm. This time the break proved to be very fortunate for me – if there is such a thing as a fortunate break.

When I broke my arm I rang Cronulla and told them the situation and asked what they wanted to do. The Sharks management said to me that, as I was unable to play due to the break, rather than fly out on a work permit it might well be better if I simply emigrated down under with my family. As they saw it, there was no hurry on their part as I was unable to play anyway until the arm healed. It was not a case of finish playing with Saints, hop on a plane and the following weekend turn out for the Sharks. The broken arm saw to that.

So I set in motion the process to emigrate with my family and worked with the club to get it done as soon as possible. That was what we eventually did, thankfully, because whilst I was settling down in Cronulla after emigrating, Great Britain joined the EU. Having joined the rest of Europe, the government then placed an embargo on transferring money out of the country by individuals, so had I not actually emigrated, I would not have been able to get my money out of the country. As it was, I had to write to the Bank of England telling them I had emigrated and settled in Australia in order to get permission from them to get my money transferred over to Sydney.

People have often asked me why I brought Cliff over to Cronulla and I tell them all the same thing, to look after me! Cliff was never a dirty player but, as a scrummaging prop forward, he was probably the best around at that time.

He was very strong and also very quick. His ball skills were not the best but his defence was outstanding. While we had a good young pack we just needed that little bit extra, and Cliff gave us that. When he was in the team we were treated a lot better by the opposition. Other teams knew that if they wanted it rough and tough there was no one better than Cliff and that we could now respond with interest. It simply let our young players know that there was the support in place if the going got tough. They also knew that the opposition respected us more when Cliff was on the field.

Tommy Bishop, St. Helens and Cronulla

Once I got to Cronulla I was able to train but I was not able to play until my arm healed. That was both a change and a shock to me I can tell you. Back in England I was never a great trainer, but when you think I was throwing 36 gallon barrels of beer around all day that weighed around 380 pounds or so, and playing at least twice a week, is it any wonder I did not like training? I did what I felt was necessary for me to stay match fit. When Tommy Bishop got hold of me he made me train and run, so much so I told him, 'Tommy have you brought me over here to play rugby or run in the bloody Melbourne Cup?'

I remember when Cliff arrived at the club and we were running around the local golf course in a training session and he was not best pleased. He sure did not like that, or the road runs we used to have to do. I think he considered himself to be a footballer, not a race horse! He was never short of effort on the field though when it was needed

Ronnie Turner, Cronulla hooker

I had never run so much in training in my life as I did when I joined the Sharks. Tommy turned up for training one night and handed me a pair of running spikes, 'We are doing 100 yard sprints tonight, six of them,' he said.

'Tommy I am not wearing them, I will bloody stab myself to death, and while you might be doing six sprints I am doing one!' But that was Tommy, he never asked anyone to do something he would not do himself. That was why he was a great on field coach. Off the field it was a different story.

> *I had waited a long time but now I was in a position to make the bugger train. The training was a lot stricter in Australia than back home. When I became coach I introduced a lot of things that were not happening at the club. I brought in sprint training sessions that I had learned from Joe Coan when I was at Saints. I also brought in a lot of Gym sessions, again from Joe's time back home. Cliff complained a bit, well he complained a bloody lot, but he did it all. In all my time playing with Cliff I never saw him run as much in training as he did at Cronulla.*

Tommy Bishop, St. Helens and Cronulla

I got two sponsorship deals when I arrived at Cronulla, the first was from Adidas who contacted me and I got a free track suit, one pair of boots a season and $100 a year cash! The second was from a company who were hired to promote milk for the Australian Milk Corporation. It had become known that before I played a game in England, I would always have a glass of milk with a couple of raw eggs mixed in. It was something unheard of in Australia. When the promotion company found out they made contact with me and the deal they offered was simple. Every time I mentioned milk when I was interviewed the company paid me $500. It was a nice deal at the time but it doesn't compare with the sponsorship payments players get paid these days, but I guess that's how the game has evolved.

It is funny how perceptions of you as a player change as your career progresses. As I have said, I never thought of myself as a ball-playing front row, I was more a head-down, arse-up, run at them sort of guy. I think, as I learned the game more, I did develop an ability to slip a pass out in the tackle but I was no Brian McTigue or Artie Beetson. You can imagine my surprise and delight when, soon after arriving, I got a write up in *Rugby League World* and the reporter wrote: 'Toughness is not Watson's only asset on the football field, he has the front row craft down to a fine art. He is a clever footballer who can set up a man with a deft pass as easily as he can destroy an opposition move with a crushing tackle.'

I think I started to believe the publicity and it certainly alerted the Penrith players when I played them in my first game for the club.

The other thing that was strange to me was that, for the first time, I was not playing in a team packed with experienced international players. Tommy had a team of youngsters who were very good players but needed leading around the pitch. When I got to the club I found that none of the players resented me, which I thought they might. I was coming into the club and earning big money and I suppose there was a risk the other players may well have thought, 'he is earning the big bucks let him do all the work.' That never happened, in fact the opposite happened, all the players had a great respect for me. One incident summed up the attitude the players had towards me when, early on in my time at Cronulla, we went to Parramatta Stadium – what was back then the Cumberland Oval – to play the Eels.

In the run up to the game I had suffered a corked calf in training and could not get it right. I decided that I would not play as I could hardly walk, let alone run. One of the lads, John McGuire, asked me if I was going to play and I told him that I was not able to get around the park. He said, 'Look Cliff, just put the shirt on and get out on the park and tell us what we have to do, I will do your work for you and also your tackling, but we really need you out on the paddock to tell us where to go and what to do.' That summed up the attitude the players had.

When I was on the pitch I used to shout and bawl at my players to get them to where they should be. I never wore a mouth guard as I would not have been able to shout at the players or abuse the bloody referees. I remember vividly on one occasion we had let in a soft try. As we stood behind the sticks I was giving the lads hell, I was effing and blinding at the top of my voice when I suddenly realised you could hear a pin drop as I was letting the boys know what I thought about their efforts. The crowd had gone silent waiting for the conversion attempt and all they could hear was me giving it rock on!

When I got to Australia and started playing week in and week out, what struck me was the game was far more violent than it ever was back in England. Back home you could expect to get a broken nose or a cauliflower ear for your troubles if you got into a blue, but generally speaking there was not much damage done. In Australia I soon found out that late tackles were being made and punches thrown when you did not have the ball. The referees seemed to have no real control of the players, but to be fair to them, the way the game was played did not help them. In Australia players ran at the man rather than at the gaps and they seemed always to rely on brawn rather than brains, which soon led to the violence. The referees seemed reluctant to take action against players and let go a great deal that English referees would have punished.

I found also the half time ritual in Australia was different. Over in England, when you went in at half time there was always a pot of tea and cup so you got a hot drink if you wanted one. In Aus it was oranges, orange juice and cold flannels to wipe your face and body down. At the time I was also a smoker, and when we played at home, the guy who managed the dressing room door always had a fag in his mouth. He would open the door for us and as I went through I would have a couple of drags on his fag before I went in! I suppose the climate dictated the differences but it took a bit of getting used to.

The next thing I found out was the competitive nature of the game down under. There was never an easy game. Back in England you could play Wigan one week and have a hard time of it, but the following game would be against the likes of Liverpool City and you got an easy ride. That was not the case in Sydney where every game was a hard one. The other thing that hit home was just how hard the pitches were and when you got tackled and hit the ground you bounced so your hips, knees and elbows took a hammering. Quite a number of the pitches had a cricket square in the middle and they were even harder and meant that you bounced even higher.

I had played against Cliff over in England in the World Cup in 1970 and he was a hard, tough bugger. When he arrived at the club it was wonderful for me as he and Graham Bowen brought a great deal of weight, and more importantly, strength into the pack. I had copped a lot of floggings as hooker playing in a lightweight pack. Hooking was an art and you spent most of the time in the scrum smashing heads with the opposition trying to win the loose head. I remember on one occasion playing up at North Sydney and I got the shit punched out of me every scrum. When I came off the field, one eye was closed and the other was fast closing as well. Even the ref asked me how my head was.

Cliff was so strong both mentally and physically and nothing worried him. He certainly looked after me once he arrived as there were very few that would dare to have a dig at me when he was around. If they did then you can bet retribution would be quick and paid back with interest. I have a great deal of respect for the guy on and off the field.

Ronnie Turner, Cronulla hooker

Mind you I did not get the best of starts to my Cronulla career as, in my first game, I copped for an injury. We were playing Penrith up at the foot of the Blue Mountains and, in the first half, instead of playing my usual head-down, arse-up style, I thought I would become a bit of a ball player as the Rugby League press had described me as one when I arrived. I took a ball up to the line and, as I tried to slip a pass out round the back of the tackler, I stuck my chin out. The Aussies needed no second chance and the next thing I knew I had copped an elbow in the jaw which of course broke. In the dressing room at half time when the doctor was assessing the damage and gave me the news, I said to him, 'Can you get someone to ring the wife and tell her to put the T-bone steak back in the freezer as I don't think I can manage it tonight'. I never tried to be a ball player again, far too dangerous.

After that I tended to slip the ball out in the tackle after I had protected my noggin!

One thing that I thought was stupid when I went over to Australia was that there were three games played on the pitch in the one day. So by the time the first grade teams got out to play, the grounds were badly cut up. Also when you finished the game and got back to the dressing rooms they were like a pig sty. The other thing to remember was that you actually trained on the playing pitch which was something that never happened at Saints. There the groundsman would not let you even walk on the pitch, let alone train on it. The guy even nailed up the door at the end of the sprint track to make sure we could not get on the field. At Saints you played on the field at three o'clock on a Saturday and no other time.

Back in my day the playing surfaces were nowhere near as good as they are today. Now with the improvements in technology and maintenance, the fields are immaculate and like a billiard table. That was not the case back in the 1970s. When first grade went out to play the field could be badly cut up and rutted.

While I'm on the subject of grounds, I have to say that, while the Sydney Cricket Ground is a great stadium with a superb heritage, it is a crap ground to play a game of Rugby League on. Because the ground is designed for cricket and a great big circular place, the supporters are miles away from the game, so there is very little atmosphere for the players. The fans cannot hear the action on the field and the players themselves hear very little of the crowd noise. In England you could hear every bloody insult the opposition fans hurled at you, but in Australia it was just a deathly silence. Also the centre of the pitch was the cricket square which was like playing on bloody concrete. If you got tackled on that it bloody hurt.

Just like there were in England, there were some hard nuts playing the game down in Sydney. John O'Neill and John Sattler could go a bit, as could the likes of Noel 'Ned' Kelly and Bob O'Reilly. I played against Bob or 'The Bear' as he was nicknamed when we played Parramatta and set my stall out to let him know I was on the field. On a number of occasions I just hit him right and knocked him back two or three yards each time. To me I had simply done what I got paid for but the press made a great thing about how I had tamed The Bear which was rubbish. Bob was a great player and one the whole game respected. These were players who had earned their reputations, just like me. They could play it any way you wanted those lads.

The Manly boys were always tough and they did not mind giving you a smack in the mouth whether you deserved it or not. John Raper was another tough bugger to play against. I found that the level of competition down under had gone up a notch or two on the game back in England. The trouble was that the hard grounds made the game faster so you got hit harder than you did playing in the winter back home.

The one thing that struck me most forcibly was that, in the Aussie game, professionalism began and ended with the money side of things. We had to carry our own playing gear with us to the games in a kit bag. After the game we had to take it home and wash it ourselves. At Saints you turned up for a game and all your kit was hanging up on a peg ready for you. After the game you threw your kit into the middle of the floor and it was collected, washed and made ready for the next game. That was not the case in Australia. You even had to drive yourself to and from away games on a Saturday as there was no team coach laid on for the players. I know that Tommy Bishop for one away game laid on a coach so the players could all travel to the game together but I do not think the board liked to pay the cost, particularly as we lost that day, so it never happened again.

Two incidents I can remember that highlight what I am talking about happened in 1972. The first occurred when at a home game Bobby Wear, the former Barrow player, came into the dressing room complaining to me about the new rules the club had introduced. When I asked him what he was talking about it seemed that all the players had only been issued with one ground pass, the pass was normally to be used to get a player into the ground when they were playing away. As we were playing at home, Bobby had given his to his wife to get into the ground. When he arrived the steward would not let him in and he actually had to pay to get into the ground to play! Can you imagine something like that happening in England?

The second event was that very same thing happened to me and I was captain of the team! When the steward told me I had to pay as I had no pass, I told him in choice language that he better get hold of the CEO as I was about to get into my car and go home and the team would be playing a man short if he continued to tell me I had to pay to get into the ground to play. In the end he backed down and let me in. I think he realised I was serious and may well have let him have one on the nose before going to my car. Incidents like that would never happen in England. To me the Aussie clubs seemed not to put the player first in all things and common sense seemed to be in short supply at times.

> *I was delighted when Cliff joined the club. I thought it was brilliant that another Englishman was in the side. When he arrived I thought the club was really going somewhere. He took on responsibility for the forwards and did a good job. All the pack was just glad to follow him. I remember that his constant theme was that he said 'We forwards fight for the ball and you backs waste the ball'.*
>
> *We had a hard season when we made the Grand Final. Cliff was in a large part responsible for that and the younger players respected him on and off the field. He was also right when he said that professionalism began and ended with the money side of things. I did give my pass to my wife one game and had to pay to get into the ground to play which was a stupid situation. I was a professional and had to pay to play!*

Bobby Wear, Cronulla and Barrow

We had a bit of success at the end of that first season at Cronulla in the Thiess Toyota Cup. This was a competition that Toyota put on for those clubs who had won nothing that season. They put up a $3,000 winner-takes-all pot and we won the thing. We beat Canterbury in the Final. The club got the $3,000 but they did put $1,500 of it into the fund for the players' end of season trip away. I think it was Dave Cotter who sat down and worked out that given the number of games we played to win the cup, and the $1,500 the club gave us for playing, it worked out that we had played each game for around $15 a man! People forget also that in that 1971 season, my first at Cronulla, we were only one win away from making the play-offs. We would probably have done so had Tommy Bishop not snapped an Achilles tendon late in the season. We had been going well at the business end of the season, but simply could not cope with the loss of our general and play maker given that we were a team short on experience. I think it was a pretty good effort considering the club had only joined the competition in 1967.

Tommy had to go back to England to get the Achilles tendon repaired and was away for a year or so. While he was away, it was more or less left up to myself and Kevin Hogan to hold the team together in 1972 until he got back. The board asked me to contribute in Tommy's absence, which I was happy to do. I was appointed captain and Kevin and I took on the coaching duties. Just the two of us back then, not like today. Now clubs have got more bloody coaches than players – head coach, assistant head coaches, defence coaches, attack coaches, goal-kicking coaches, touch-kicking coaches, cycling coaches – the list is endless. It is no wonder the Aussie clubs are going broke. Without the sponsorship money and television money the clubs would have gone to the wall. They certainly would not survive on the money people pay through the turnstiles to watch the games.

*****

In the 1972 season we went backwards a little, simply because we were missing Tommy in my opinion. He was out of the game for over a year as he recovered from the Achilles injury. We finished well down the table that year and did not make the play-off finals, but the following season was a different story altogether. Tommy returned to the club and the youngsters had a little more experience after being together for a couple of seasons, and we started to go well in the competition. We seemed to do a lot of things right and we beat all of the big boys. At the midpoint of the season we won six straight games, and in the run in to the finals we won our last five league games. We won 17 of our 22 league games and got second place on the ladder. Manly actually took top spot with 35 and we had 34. We had three Brits in the side at the time: myself, Tommy and Bobby Wear.

I have a photo of the Cronulla front row getting ready to pack down, and in the photo is Mick Naughton, the referee from Widnes. It was in 1973 and a few weeks before the finals. I think it was the first time that an English referee came down to Australia to referee games and we played St. George at the Sydney Cricket Ground when he was in the middle with the whistle. That afternoon we lost that game against St. George 15-10. But a few weeks later we got our revenge beating them 18-0 and it was the first time ever that St. George had failed to score a point when playing at the SCG. It is a little record the Cronulla club have. I think it is still the case even today.

The reason why Mick Naughton came down was, I think, in an attempt to make the then New South Wales versus Queensland games a little more attractive to the supporters. In 1973 the state games were dying on their feet and the authorities brought an English referee over to attract a little attention. The games were played at Lang Park up in Brisbane mid-week so as not to interfere with the league fixtures. Mick refereed two state games, New South Wales winning both of them. Before he returned home he was given a club game to make the trip worthwhile I suppose, and we got him. It was a little strange to go back to being refereed properly by a Pommie referee. I remember he was talking to the players all through the game, refereeing as he ran, it was great.

Everyone at the club was excited as, for the first time in the club's short six-year existence, we had made the play-off finals. I felt that I had justified my decision to leave Saints to play in the Sydney competition. The thing was that we had not won anything yet, but the younger players were just delighted to be in the play-offs. All of the play-off games back then were played at the Sydney Cricket Ground which, like I've said, is a magnificent place historically but it's no Wembley, that's for sure.

With the exception of Tommy and myself, none of the other players had experienced sudden death football which was what the play-off was, although by finishing in second spot we did earn ourselves a second bite of the cherry which, as it turned out, we needed. During the season we played Manly twice and won and lost one. When we beat them toward the end of the season there was a bit of bad blood stirred up between a number of our players and Mal Reilly, well a lot of bad blood to be honest. Mal was no shrinking violet and liked to put it about a bit himself. The bad blood was to get worse during the play-off finals.

We won through to the Grand Final beating both St. George and Newtown to do so, having lost to Manly in the minor final. It was in that game that the bad blood that had developed between the two teams came to the fore once again. During our game against Manly at Endeavour Field, our hooker Ronnie Turner and Mal Reilly had a series of dust-ups. The end result was that Ronnie copped an elbow from Mal in a late tackle and needed 28 stitches in a mouth wound. He was determined to square up come the Grand Final, and boy did he.

When we were running up to the Final in that week, there was certainly a lot more pomp and ceremony than back home for a Wembley Final. Back in England, because the Challenge Cup Final is played down in the capital, you are away from all the hype back in St. Helens and the Londoners don't have a clue what is happening anyway. But the lack of professionalism in the Aussie game off the field really did show itself on the big match day.

Back home when we got to the Wembley Final, I remember all the wives and girlfriends of the Saints players were put on a train down to Wembley on the Saturday morning and had the best seats in the stadium to watch the game. After the game when we left the dressing room and walked onto the team bus in the tunnel at the stadium, the ladies were already sitting on the coach and we all went to the hotel for the celebrations. Compare that to what happened in Australia when Cronulla got to the Grand Final. I actually drove to the match at the Sydney Cricket Ground in my car from Miranda where I lived, and Barbara my wife had to pay to get into the ground to watch the game from the 'Hill'. The club didn't even purchase stand tickets for the wives and girlfriends to sit in to watch the game; in fact they did not buy any tickets full stop. That was the biggest example of the unprofessionalism and stupidity of clubs I spoke of earlier. Can you imagine an English club letting players make their own way to the ground when they were playing an important game?

The other thing to remember is that all the players were used to playing at the SCG so it was not a special place for them. Every week the authorities would select a 'match of the day' which would be televised and it was always played at the ground. It was a bit of a Saturday ritual for supporters to go down to the Bat and Ball pub and get a skin full. They would then somehow get their tinnies inside the ground and throw beer over everybody and then throw the empty cans at the players. The Grand Final was not even special to the supporters really for that very same reason given they went there most Saturdays. Wembley on the other hand was the 'holy grail', players felt it was a privilege to play on that pitch. There was nothing special for the players about playing at the SCG.

A lot has been written about that Grand Final in 1973 and it being the dirtiest of all time, but we did not really want to play the game that way. Tommy did admit much later that it was his intention to upset the rhythm of the Manly side, and he felt that the only way to do so was to cause mayhem, and he did that in spades. It is funny how myths develop and perpetuate and I am involved in one or two myself.

During the warm up prior to the kick off in the Final, I spent most of the time leaning against the post while others were jogging around or doing press ups. On being approached by Tommy I supposedly said, 'Don't worry Tommy, they have not kicked off yet.' Nothing like that happened. The truth is that prior to the game I had damaged three rib cartilages and so had a pain killing injection from the doctor before we went out. I was leaning on the posts simply trying not to damage the ribs before I had to during the match. It made little difference because the first time I carried the ball up, John O'Neill whacked me right in the ribs. He got me just right so the injection was of little use.

Once the Grand Final did start there was the usual softening up period, but it seemed to last for the whole of the first half and well into the second half. What people who write about that game seem to forget was that it was Cronulla that kicked off and Manly, when they got the ball, kicked it straight back to us. So if any team wanted to cause mayhem it was Manly, and they were determined to have first go. Ronnie Turner had set his sights on Mal Reilly and early on in the game Mal took the ball from acting half, then as he began running away from the ruck he put up a bomb. As Mal put boot to ball, Ronnie launched himself at him and hit him with a Duggie Greenall type tackle – he hit Mal square on with his shoulder, his hips, his knees, the lot. He was just like a cannonball and Mal went down with a hip and knee injury that eventually put him out of the game – but not before he had created a bit more mayhem.

In a game earlier in the season, Mal Reilly had hit Ronnie with an elbow up at Endeavour Field and Ronnie needed around 30 stitches in a mouth wound. Ronnie discharged himself from the hospital and came back to the club looking for Mal. When he found him he told him, 'You're in my little black book mate and I am going to get you'. In the final he evened the score early in the game and Mal had to leave the field for a needle. When he came back onto the field, Cliff shouted across to him in that broad Pommie accent as he took his place in the Manly defensive line, 'Okay lad, I know what you are up to so do not try it'.

Ken Maddison, Cronulla second-row

In that final the truth is that, rather than targeting Mal Reilly, we would have done far better concentrating on Bobby Fulton and shutting him down. He won the game for Manly as the bugger turned up in the wrong place at the wrong time – for us that is – not once but twice. He scored the two tries that eventually won the game for his side and left us feeling sorry for ourselves.

Tommy, true to his word, was niggling and worrying at every opportunity, and on one carry I took a pass and drove the ball up. On looking up I saw Reilly coming to tackle me and I knew what was coming, an elbow, so I dropped my shoulder and ducked under Mal's swinging arm as he came in to hit me and put me down on the floor. While we both were on the ground following the tackle, Mal grabbed hold of my shirt and stopped me getting up to play the ball. I was just going to belt him when he said, 'Stay where you are Cliff, there's a bit of a blue going on up top.' When I turned and looked up off the ground, all around us there were bodies and scuffles and punches being thrown, so we both lay there and watched the action. Tommy carried on creating mayhem but in the end we just failed to get over the line. People felt that had the game gone on a little longer, with all the pressure we were exerting we could have won the Final.

We did have one chance to win in the last few minutes of the game. We ran a move called 'flick' which involved Tommy, myself and Ronnie Turner. We had run the move in previous games that season, including against Manley, with some success. Tommy decided to alter the move slightly for the Final so that it may well fool the Manly defence in the game. Late on when we were on the attack, Tommy called it before we were really set and both Ronnie and I were a little unsighted. Also our second-row ran a line for the old move forgetting we had changed it. The result was that the three of us went for the ball at the same time. If Ronnie or I had actually caught the ball that Tommy popped up, then we would have scored as a massive gap had opened up in the Manly defence. The problem was I knocked the ball on and the chance was lost. As I said, I was never a ball handling prop forward!

After the match we were critisised by the press for the way the game had been played, but Manly were not exactly innocent either. One reporter felt the game was as dirty as any bar room brawl. Even the great John Raper said it was the most disgraceful game of football he had ever witnessed.

A lot has been said about that match, but in the dressing room before we went out I said to the players, 'Let's play our game, but if it is on then let's give as good as we get'. I think Manly thought we would not respond but they were wrong. We should have won that Final but in the last five minutes or so we were losing 10-7 and got a penalty but two points were no good to us at that stage. When we ran the move, Ian Martin was miles offside, but the referee did not give us another penalty. We really should have contained Bobby Fulton but he was such a great player and won the game for Manly.

I have been lucky enough to play in a Final at the Sydney Cricket Ground and also at Wembley, and believe me there is no comparison. There is nothing that beats Wembley Stadium, for a player it is fabulous. I was lucky enough to win at Wembley and also watch my son, Paul, play there for Warrington, but sadly he was on the losing side that afternoon.

Tommy Bishop, St. Helens and Cronulla

I copped a bit of flak from the Aussie press who had not forgotten the 'Liverpool kiss' incident, and this time they had proof. They published a photograph of me belting Peter Peters with a left hook, but at the time Peter was clutching at his groin. His hands were a long way from where they should have been and it looked for all the world that I had 'king hit' him, which is a term the Aussies use to describe a punch that is thrown when the receiver is not looking or aware. Now I have never been that sort of player; when I hit someone it was because they had hit me and they knew bloody well that a punch was coming back. In all of my career I never threw a punch when I was making a tackle on a player or when a player was not looking.

The reporters had a field day after the game, giving it to me good and proper. When I saw the photograph in the paper I couldn't figure out why he was holding his crown jewels, because if I had hit him he would have been holding his jaw. It is a question I have asked myself since that game. In that time I have been asked countless times why, when I smacked Peter in the chops, was he clutching his bollocks. I finally found out the answer to the question in September 2013, almost 40 years to the day, when I was at a Men of League function and they had organised a reunion of the Manly and Sharks teams that played in the Grand Final back in 1973.

While I was at the function, I went up to Peter for a chat and asked him just why he was clutching his crotch when I was supposedly swinging at him. His answer was very simple. He looked at me with a twinkle in his eye and said, 'Tommy Bishop had just kicked me in the bollocks.' For 40 years I had copped the flak from both the press and supporters and it was Tommy who was to blame and not me for seemingly king hitting poor old Peter.

> *When Cliff arrived at the club, we had a lightweight pack compared to a lot of the other clubs. He was an established international with a reputation to match and he gave us strength in the scrum. He was able to hold the opposition pack and pull them around to allow us to win the football in what were contested scrums back then. He also strengthened our blindside defence to such an extent that we became one of the best defensive teams in the comp. He was never a workaholic off the paddock, but on it had a great reputation, and he was a very cool customer. In the 1973 Grand Final, in the few minutes prior to kick off when everyone is tense, Cliff was stood leaning on the goal post waiting for the game to start. I have the greatest admiration for Cliff and what he achieved in the game.*

Greg Pierce, Cronulla and former Australian captain

After the game we thought our season was over, but there had been plans for the Australian Champions to play the New Zealand Champions. I suppose it was a precursor for today's World Club Challenge. The New Zealand Champions were the Ponsonby Ponies but Manly refused the invitation, so the sponsors, Four Roses Bourbon, asked Cronulla if they would like to play and we went like a shot.

Tommy Bishop, Chris Wellman, Grahame Bowen and I went over early to promote the 'Grand Slam' game, as it was dubbed, for which the sponsors had put up $6,000, winner take all. When we got there Bowen, who worked in the CID in Sydney, met up with a policeman who was on a stakeout job. When he found out who we were he said to Bowen, 'Bugger the job, I can do that tomorrow'.

The copper took us out on the piss that evening and, while we were in a bar, there was a talk show on the radio and callers were saying how the Ponsonby side were going to beat Cronulla, pointing out we could not beat Manly. The copper took exception to this so piled us all into a taxi and we rolled up at the radio station, went in and chatted to the host on air. I walked out of the studio to go to the toilet and could not find my way back, so decided to go back to the hotel. I was got up out of bed by the lads when they returned and we all went down to the bar which was still open. We asked the barman to make us every cocktail he had ever made which was a big mistake as he had worked on the liner The Queen Elizabeth. I forget what happened after that.

When matchday arrived the rest of the team were supposed to fly into Auckland the night before, but their flight was diverted to Wellington due to bad weather. They all travelled up by road and arrived having been on the piss for the whole journey. When the match kicked off we were all worse for wear. I remember I dropped three passes and they scored three tries. At half time the score was 26-0 and in the dressing room Bish went ape and shoved us all into the cold shower to sober us up. The second half we played like we could do but lost the game 28-26!

When the Final was over and my contract was coming to a close, I went to see the board to discuss the options in the contract, but they were not prepared to come to the party. I had it written in the contract that the club had an option on me for 1974 and 1975 and I really felt I had another two years at the very top level in me. A few weeks before the Grand Final I had been asked to do a bit of coaching with the Wollongong Wolves down in the Illawarra. I coached the forwards and the club won their last four games. The Sharks board got to hear about it and I am not sure if that affected their thinking. Back then when players left the Sydney Competition they almost always went to play 'bush' Rugby League, and a number of former Sharks players were at Wollongong at the time. That was why I was approached by the club to help out with the forwards.

There was a second-row named Fred Tomlinson, who had played for Barrow back home, who came over to play for the Sharks, but he objected about having to push in the scrum; he kept insisting that he was a ball handler not a scrummager. He finished up playing at Wollongong as he could not get into first grade. They also had a great old player by the name of Hal Browne as player/coach at the time. They had some good players in that side. I enjoyed my time coaching and I suppose it whetted my appetite for a move into that area. I also knew that Tommy had a job for life with the Sharks if he wanted it, so I would have to move if I wanted a player/coaching job.

I think the board sort of felt I was wanting to move in that direction, so when we sat down to discuss options they were not very helpful. I told them that I wanted $10,000 a year plus match payments if I was to re-sign for the club. I also told them that despite being 33 years old, I felt I had two or three more good seasons left in me. After all I had got the club to a Grand Final and was playing as well as I ever had. They of course were reluctant to pay that but eventually they came round to my way of thinking. What stopped the whole deal was that I wanted a three year contract, just like the one I had signed that brought me out from England. They would not agree to that, even though I felt that I still had three more seasons left in me.

It was crazy really, we had a young team and we had just got to the Grand Final. Not only that, we had almost beaten the Manly side that was the millionaire club at the time. The board, either from a lack of ambition or a lack of courage, simply could not or would not build on that success. I know the authorities had brought in a rule stating that a club could only pay a player $2,000 to sign for the club and they could not pay more than $200 per game, but few if any of the clubs abided by that rule. Sadly Cronulla felt, or a certain member of the board felt, they had to and so the team was allowed to disintegrate.

> We had an idiot in a senior position at the club at that time who was more interested in sucking up to League headquarters rather than doing what was best for his club. He did not have the interests of the club at heart and kept saying that we couldn't break the rules but almost every other club was doing just that. I could have got Bob McCarthy to come to the club, but that idiot would not pay the extra $500 needed to get him to sign. I told the man he could pick up the $500 off the floor of the club in dropped change to get Bob to join. The daft thing was that a car dealer in the town was willing to pay Bob so it would have cost the club nothing, but no, he said they could not break the rules. When I challenged him he told me that he could cancel my contract, so I told the idiot to do so as I knew Manly wanted to sign me. The guy was a complete idiot and not interested in the club and the team was allowed to literally fade away.

> Ronnie Turner, Cronulla Hooker

I know for a fact that one Manly player was actually on a contract worth $15,000 dollars a year, which was most definitely breaking the rules. But Cronulla, for whatever reason, were not prepared to do the same. So for a lack of ambition, the club lost the chance of dominating the competition for the next few years. The young players were getting more and more experienced and Tommy and I could have continued guiding them around the park. Who knows what we could have achieved. I really believe that the club could have gone on to bigger and better things. After all we had almost won a Grand Final and the same players had remained with the club; we had gained a great deal of respect and other clubs were now wary of playing against us. There is no way of knowing what we could have gone on to achieve the following two or three seasons. It just shows how an individual in a position of authority at a club can make or break a side!

> *Cliff was right about the team breaking up. I was coming to the end of my career and, after the Grand Final, I followed Cliff down to Wollongong. I played there for a season. It would have been nice to see just what the club could have achieved but it was not to be. Tommy left and so did Cliff and I and others followed later on. The drive had gone from the club.*

> *Bobby Wear, Cronulla and Barrow.*

When it became known that the club were stalling, Wollongong Wolves came in and offered me the player/coach job. The existing coach Hal Brown was happy and said that he would stay with the club if I would take on the coaching role. I told them that I was taking my wife on a world cruise and I would give them an answer once I got back to Australia. With that Barbara and I went off for a good long holiday. When we arrived in England I actually went up to Leeds to watch the first Test and, while I was there, I met up with some of the Saints players.

I went over to St. Helens and saw Basil Lowe and Harry Cook. I told them I was a free agent and asked if they wanted to sign me again. They were keen until I told them what I was looking for. I asked for £50 per game win, lose or draw for the short time I would be in the country and available to them. The club was having a bit of a lean time of it then and I thought it was a reasonable offer. They nearly collapsed in front of me saying there was no way they could afford that. I told them that I would put 3,000 on the first home gate I played for the club. Half of the spectators would turn up just so they could say that the club should never have transferred me and the other half so they could say the club was right to get shut of me when they did! The upshot was that I carried on with the holiday.

While I was on the ship on the way over to England, the radio officer, who was a big rugby fan and used to listen in to radio hams, stopped me one day and told me that Tommy Bishop had left Cronulla and signed for Norths up in Brisbane in Queensland. I did not believe him but decided to investigate a bit further. I found out that while I'd been away, the Cronulla board told Tommy that they had to abide by the new signing fee and match payment rulings. Tommy had told the club there was no way he was playing for that and had buggered off. So by following the rules, which few if any other clubs were doing, the club also lost its coach that had taken them to their first Grand Final.

*After the Final, I sat down with the board to negotiate a
new player/coach deal. In the 1973 season I had earned
$15,000, which was a good deal of money for that time. I
felt that I should at least be on the same salary for the 1974
season. Sadly the club was being badly run at that time.
Several of the club officials were not willing to pay me
what I'd already been earning, so I decided I'd had enough
and I left for Norths up in Brisbane.*

*The club had lost Monty Porter, the secretary, who
was a great friend to me. Had he still been around, I reckon
that team and the club would have gone on to bigger and
better things. As it was the team was allowed to drift apart.
Cliff was not offered a new deal and the whole thing just
disintegrated.*

Tommy Bishop, St. Helens and Cronulla

With Tommy gone, the club was in need of a coach and
they contacted me while I was still travelling and offered
me the player/coach role. It was while I was up at Leeds
watching the Test match. Bob Abbott and Arthur Wynn
from the club were at the game and they told me what
had happened and asked if I would coach the side. I am
a man of my word and told them what I had said to
the Wollongong officials and that I would not make a
decision until I got back home and had talked to them.

Perhaps I was wrong and should have taken the
Cronulla job as I am sure Wollongong would have
appreciated my position, but that was not the way I
worked. Cronulla felt they did not want to wait that
long as they needed to prepare for the upcoming season.
They appointed Noel Thornton, a former captain of the
club, as the new coach. So when I got home the only
offer on the table was the Wollongong one as player/
coach which I took.

Getting back home to Australia proved to be more of a problem than I expected. I tried to rent a house in St. Helens and could not do so for love nor money. In the end I said to my wife, 'That's it we are going back to Australia'. Then I tried to book a flight but at the time, in December 1974, there was an energy crisis and the earliest I could get a flight was weeks ahead. I asked if they had any cancellations and, unbelievably, there was a flight with seats for me, my wife and children flying out on Christmas Eve! We all took the flight and spent Christmas Day in Bombay – not the best place to be to spend such a holiday.

That was how I arrived in the Illawarra with the Wolves. People need to remember that back in the 1970s the Illawarra competition was very strong. The area had a great reputation for producing players that would go on and play for their country. Also there were a lot of players who could have played in the Sydney comp but for whatever reasons, travel, time, family commitments, chose to stay and play down in the Illawarra. Players like David Waite who would coach Great Britain, Mick Cronin, John Dorahy and the likes all started their careers in the Illawarra competition.

I had just broken into the Wests first grade team at the tender age of 17 and our coach, Warren Ryan, approached Cliff to come down and have a session with our front row. And boy did he give them a session. He had our props lifted up, pulled down, twisted around until they had no idea if it was Monday or Tuesday. They could hardly walk by the time he had finished but he told them this is what you need to be able do to reach the top level.

John Dorahy, Wests and Hull KR

I had a great time down with the Wollongong club and my plan was that, having got a three year deal, I would spend the first season trying to develop a team that would do well in the competition and get away from the bottom of the table. If I did that then the second and third seasons we could try to win the comp with the team built during that first year.

The players when I arrived really responded well to the coaching and the training. The mixture of old heads and young legs seemed to gel almost at once. That plan I had put in place went out of the window as in that first year at the Wolves we won the Minor Premiership, coming top of the table. The previous season I think the club had been in the bottom three. We just seemed to play well and play consistently through the season, and at the end of the campaign I found myself playing in another Grand Final, this time down in the Illawarra. Sadly the result was the same as, despite being expected to win, Corrimal pipped us 22 to 8 and I had lost two Grand Finals in two years.

Whilst my international playing days were over, or so I thought, fate intervened and I was given one last hurrah. This time I would be playing against Great Britain rather than for them. I was selected to captain the Illawarra Southern District side to play the touring side in 1974. The tourists had lost the Ashes and we were the last team they would play before moving over to New Zealand. I told my players that the Great Britain side really had nothing to play for and so we could well cause an upset if we really dug in when we played them. That was what we did and we almost turned them over. We were 15-10 down at half time but in the end Great Britain had too many big guns and they won the game

I think 26-22. I remember Steve Nash dropped a goal which showed how desperate they were that afternoon. It was nice to get one last shot at international football and I really enjoyed myself in that game.

I played for Great Britain against Cliff and the Illawarra district team in 1974. Cliff was a big, strong, tough prop. You can tell the strength of a player when you have to tackle him and Cliff was strong. You needed to work bloody hard, even when you got hold of Cliff such was his strength. He was not a dirty player and neither was he a bully, he was just one of those players that could and would look after himself and his team-mates. Funnily enough I did not play against him that often over in England but we faced each other in that Illawarra game at the end of the Australian leg of the tour. He could make you smile on the field could Cliff; during that game the ball was on the other side of the field and as Cliff passed me he shouted, 'Get over there where the bloody ball is Jim.' I told him 'You get over there.' His quick reply was, 'You are the one playing for Great Britain not me.' There is little doubt in my mind Cliff was the best prop around in the world when he was in his prime.

Jim Mills, Widnes

That game was a different kettle of fish from the one played in 1970 when I was on the other side. Back then we had won the Ashes and went down to the Illawarra to play the Southern District side. As we were going out and lining up to kick off, the referee said to us that as it was the last match before we went over to New Zealand, he wanted a good clean game as he did not want to send anyone off the field. Our skipper Roger Millward said to me, 'Right Cliff, let's have some fun'. Boy did we have fun. Players like Mal Reilly did not need a second invitation and, by the end of the game, the opposition players were looking like the casualty ward at the local hospital. There were stitches and broken bones everywhere. Mind you, on the back of all the mayhem Roger scored three tries and kicked three goals and we won 24-11.

While I was at Wollongong, the all-conquering Aussies returned from the 1974 tour to England and the authorities organised a match played at Manly between them and a 'select' side. I was selected at prop and in the pack there was also Mal Reilly, Bill Ashurst and his good mate Mick Stephenson. I remember that the late, great Jack Gibson was asked to coach us but he could not work his magic as we got beaten in front of 16,000 screaming Aussie fans 26-0. It was strange because within a year I had played against both Great Britain and Australia and lost both games!

I had some good times playing down in Wollongong and I can tell you a story that shows the sort of man Jim Morgan was and what a great friend of mine he became. People only remember the Brisbane Test match of 1970 when he and I had a 'disagreement' but as I have said he became a good mate of mine. One Saturday I captained Illawarra district and we played Monaro who were captained by Jim. I said to Jim during a break in the game, 'Mate we are going to have to do something.' to which he replied, 'What are you talking about?' I said, 'Well after the battle of Brisbane, we better have another blue to get the crowd going'. Jim was in agreement and I squared it up with the ref what we were going to do. He gave us the nod to go ahead and do it and was prepared when it happened.

As we formed up for a scrum I nodded to Jim and

to the ref, and as we packed down Jim and I suddenly erupted out of the scrum and grabbed each other and started swinging but not really hitting each other. The crowd went wild on the side line and folks were screaming and cheering. The referee let it go for a while then stepped in and stopped us, wagged his finger and told us that we should scrum down again. We both packed down laughing our heads off – as was the referee – but the crowd loved it. That was the good bloke Jim was and he became a great friend of mine. I was very sad when he died I can tell you.

As is often the case, when you get a little success at a club, the board suddenly believe they know better than the coach, and Wollongong were no different. The board started to sign players for the second season without asking my opinion and did not re-sign players that I wanted at the club. They actually signed a centre that was slower than me and I ended up playing him at prop forward! As a result, we lost the momentum we had generated in that first season. We couldn't maintain the standards that that we had achieved, and while we made the final play-offs, we were not successful in getting a Grand Final spot.

The club then told me at the end of the second season that they simply could not afford to pay my contract for the third year and pay the players as well, so I told them not to worry and left. Helensburgh, who also played in the Illawarra league, contacted me and asked if I would coach them and so I tried to work out a deal with them but I found that Maurie Raper, John Raper's brother, had undercut me, so he got the job as coach. He asked if I would play for the club and I agreed. We played the first trial game against St. George and made a draw. In the second game we did not play well and at training Raper told me he was thinking of dropping me from the first grade side as I had not played well. I told him not to bother, threw my boots in the bin and told him I was retiring. I had never been dropped in all my career so was not about to experience it then.

The following season, I think it was 1976, Tommy Bishop came back down from Queensland to take up the coaching job with North Sydney. Once he returned he rang me and asked if I was willing to coach the reserve grade, so I did. Unfortunately when I got to the club I found that there was a lot of politics within the place. All sorts of folks wanted to pick the teams, some board members liked Tommy and others did not. It was all very disruptive and I was experiencing the same sort of thing in the reserve grade. I insisted on selecting my team myself, telling the board that it is the coach who takes the blame if things do not go well, not them. It did not go down well but I stuck to my guns!

I think Tommy won one or two games in first grade that season and I won about six. All the coaches in the three grades got the sack at the end of the season and I decided to call it a day with the game after that. I settled down to a life as a normal person, albeit still in Miranda where I live to this day and still support the Cronulla Sharks, although I do not always see eye to eye with things that they do.

I had been involved with the game for over 17 years and loved every moment but there is a time for every player when they need to draw the curtain down on their playing and coaching career, and I had reached mine.

5

The English Game Today

I am very proud of the fact that I played in the Great Britain team that won the Ashes in 1971. I am equally proud of the fact that we won that series in Australia. We overcame the iron-hard grounds, the heat, the odd refereeing decisions that were made and the very good Aussie sides we faced in all three Tests. What I am not proud of is that we have not won a series since that time. Since I retired I have often been asked why it is that the Aussies have moved so far ahead of the English in the playing of the game. I have my own ideas which may well not sit well with the authorities in England.

I think, first and foremost, we lost the opportunity to build on the 1971 touring side that won the Ashes. The Australian clubs came over to England and signed players of the likes of Mal Reilly, Phil Lowe and myself and that upset the system in England. We then lost players of the calibre of Mike Stephenson, Mick Adams, Bill Ashurst, Brian Lockwood and John Gray, amongst others, and those younger players who were coming through were lost to our game.

When I moved down under, we had a good mix of experienced international players and up and coming players who would take over from them. The whole future looked rosy but suddenly the whole thing was thrown out of joint. The 1974 Lions tourists to Australia were a very good outfit who simply got refereed out of a series win. They should have won the Ashes but didn't, and of course we lost Johnny Whiteley as the national coach. He was a great coach and a player's coach to boot. Johnny had done it both as a player and as a coach at international level and then he and his experience was lost to the international game.

The game deteriorated from then on back home, in my opinion for a number of reasons. Firstly the English players lacked the stamina needed to play the new style of Rugby League demanded by the six-tackle rule. Many players were much overweight to the tune of more than a few pounds at times. In the past it did not have that great an effect as in the game we used to let the ball do the work. We would run at the gaps and draw men in, allowing a pass to be made that put a player through a gap. Forwards did not really run far with the ball. There were odd ones like Dick Huddart, and even myself, who were quick for a front row forward, but generally forwards were either head-down, arse-up ball carriers or they were ball distributors who would take the ball up to the line and slip out a pass to a half back or three quarter running into a gap. The stamina level of most forwards was quite low.

You have to remember that back before the six-tackle rule came in, our game was much more methodical. A team would build up pressure on the opposition by the forwards driving the ball up the middle of the field to suck in defenders, and then the backs would work a move to try to score. If it failed then you started all over again and eventually the opposition cracked – a gap appeared here or there and a try was scored. Suddenly that methodical style of play was replaced by what I call panic football.

We had the four-tackle rule which, in truth, was not that, it was more like two tackle rugby. More often than not the scrum-half would get tackled with the ball at a scrum or the stand-off would be tackled and a team then had only two tackles to try to work something before they had to kick. We were simply not geared up to play that style of game and neither were we able to play six-tackle rugby for the same reasons. That type of rugby is far more intense, demanding greater fitness than did the unlimited tackle game.

The second problem was the influx into the English game of Australian coaches who brought with them a different style of play. Suddenly coaches wanted players to run hard and fast at the man, not the gap. They then wanted the player to get to his feet as fast as he could to play the ball. Such a game demanded even greater stamina, stamina that was not present in the English game. The game I knew simply changed overnight. Prior to the four and six-tackle rule coming in, the top try scorer was the wingman, someone like Brian Bevan with something like 70 tries in a season. During the season wingmen like Boston at Wigan, Freeman at Halifax or Tommy Voll at Saints would regularly be scoring 40 or 50 tries. When the rules changed I think Bob Haigh, a second-row forward, was top try scorer with about 21 or 22!

Teams could not plan a try and work towards scoring it, they had to simply hope for a break that would lead to a score. And the Aussie coaches felt that the best way to get such breaks was by their players running over the top of opposition players, getting up and playing the ball as quickly as possible. Playing the game at that higher speed demanded far greater stamina and fitness.

The Aussie coaches changed the way we played to try and bring us into line with what they had done with their teams back home. New defensive patterns were brought in but the English players did not adapt well because of the weight and stamina issues. So clubs and coaches brought in Aussie players – many of them second rate – who knew the system the coaches wanted the teams to play. The result was English players were replaced by imports, the game suffered greatly and our international team simply withered on the vine.

There is no doubt in my mind that the Aussies adapted better to the four and six-tackle game than we did. In England we tried to adapt our existing style of play to fit into the six tackles, whereas the Aussies didn't. They went away and totally reassessed the game of Rugby League. To them the new game was very similar to American Football with its four 'downs'. They brought in skills from American Football and they changed their training methods to ensure players developed the stamina needed to play the game at a higher speed. They increased the fitness, speed and size of their players to play the new style of rugby that the new rules required. They introduced weight training programmes to bulk up the players – all of them, not just the forwards. Sure individual players of skill emerged like Wally Lewis, Brett Kenny and Peter Sterling, but on the whole coaches coached such skills out of their teams and their players. It became the mantra to play 'error free' rugby.

In today's game it is the coach who tells the players how to play on the field, not the players actually on the field. We have right side coaches and plays and left side coaches and plays. Different plays when the team is in different parts of the field and so on. The coaches prepare a game plan that must be rigidly adhered to. The spontaneous players of my day would not fit into the present day game. Now all the players are big men, all have good speed and all have great stamina. Anyone can take the ball up from first receiver; there are no more head-down, arse-up type of players in the game. The first receiver is just as likely to be a wingman as a prop. Now when you look, all the players across the park are the same size and all have good speed.

With the six-tackle rule came other rule changes designed to speed up the game even more, supposedly to make it more exciting. The argument was that the unlimited tackles made the game boring and predictable, yet what we see today is typically five drives and a kick to the corner for the wing and centre to try and get a hand on the ball to score. Is that not boring and predictable? I think it is. We stopped having competitive scrums and we now simply use a scrum as a means of restarting a game quickly. I do a lot of work with the 'Men of League' here in Australia and last year I was with Fred Jones, the former St. George hooker, who was giving a talk and he said that most people thought Cameron Smith, the Melbourne Storm hooker, was the best hooker in the world. Fred's argument was simple: how could that be when he had never packed in a competitive scrum? I thought how very true that was. Smith would never win a ball in a competitive scrum with the likes of Bill Sayer or Bob Dagnall or any other hooker from the era of competitive scrums. More often than not he packs down in the loose forward spot anyway. He's a good player but he is not a hooker, he is simply a ball distributer who operates from dummy half, so let's not call him a hooker.

Those are some reasons for the decline of the English game but our players have also to take a lot of the blame. The players today seem to me to have lost that love of the old red, white and blue of mother England. I would have played for Great Britain for nothing, for the pride in pulling on that international shirt. Now players are crying off international games for the most trivial of reasons. 'I cannot play as my wife is expecting a baby,' or, 'I have business interests that keep me at home.' The Australians are equally to blame, they do not seem to be interested in pulling on a green and gold shirt. They are happy to play Origin but not to go to Papua New Guinea and the likes.

The English players of today have lost the hunger because the money is too easily got now. When I played, particularly at Saints, we were on £12 for a win and £7 for a loss. Before kick-off Harry Cook would come into the dressing room after weighing up the size of the crowd on the ground and say to us, 'There is a £10 bonus for the win'. So our wage packet was dependent upon the crowd we attracted. If we won we got a bigger pay packet, and winning meant the crowd kept coming back to watch us. Now players get a contract and get their money if they play or not. If I did not play in a game for whatever reason I got no money.

Equally important in my view, English players need to get more fire in their belly, get more pride in pulling on an international jersey and more pride in winning every game. The only way to beat the Aussies is for the English to get into their faces and do so from first whistle to last. Do not let them run or boss the game, play with mongrel and to hell with the consequences. Simply take the view that no Aussie is going to get past me, run over me or out muscle me. You only get that mentality if you are a hungry player, hungry for success, hungry for the win. Are the English players hungry enough to do that?

I see props in particular playing 15 minutes and then they are on the sideline riding a bloody bike for God's sake. What is that all about? They are fitter now than ever, yet cannot play 80 minutes. The game has stopped being a 13-a-side game and become a 17-a-side game which is not right. I would take it as a personnel insult if I had to come off the field after 15 or 20 minutes for a 'rest'. We have removed the fatigue factor out of the game and there is no need for a player to drive himself hard in training to ensure he lasts the full 80 minutes. More often than not they only play half a game. To some extent I think that their fitness training is geared to that fact.

The other question I am often asked is can we ever get to a stage where we can beat the Aussies. I have to say no we will not. It has nothing to do with the weather as the teams in England are now playing in the summer. We are simply five years behind the Australian trends and always will be because the game and the administration in England are stuck in a rut. Here in Australia the teams have wrestling coaches who are teaching players not only how to put a player onto the ground quickly but also how to stay on their feet longer to attract more players in to make the tackle. Then a quick play the ball will give the team an advantage. It is just coming into the game in England. We are still not playing the game to our strengths but are content to copy what is happening down under, and we regularly produce players of great creativity and they get it coached out of them. The mantra is always the same, play the man not the gap, do not think during the game but simply follow the game plan that has been practised all week in training. There is no room in the game for any player who does something 'off the cuff' anymore; the mantra says that by doing that you run away from your team-mates or spoil a move planned by the coach that is to be run when in a certain position on the field.

Also the Super League clubs seem to be only interested in making a profit. I do agree with that to some extent; clubs should pay their way and not spend money they have not got. The problem is that there is no reserve grade in the game at the top level in England and if you have not made it at the age of 20 you are out. We have the stupid situation that young players at a Super League club are farmed out to clubs in the lower leagues. I cannot really see what they are going to learn, or how they are going to improve doing that. You do not improve by playing in a lesser competition, you simply learn bad habits, nothing more. Let's get back to reserve grade and improve the quality of the reserve grade competition as that is how players will get better.

Finally I think the authorities and clubs in both countries have lost sight of their responsibilities to the game as a whole. Australia has been top of the tree now for nearly 50 years and yet has done little to develop the game outside of the NRL. Okay they may well play a game in the country and think they are spreading the word, but they are not. Country rugby in Australia or 'Bush Rugby' as it is called is dying due to a lack of funding. The game seems only to be interested in making money for the clubs. We have a massive television contract at present and all the clubs are interested in is increasing their salary cap spending with this extra cash.

Administrators for the clubs and the game generally are not interested in developing the international scene as there is no money in that for them. Better to develop the State of Origin as being the pinnacle of the game, after all that brings in far more revenue. Better to develop Super League as that is where the money is, never mind the clubs and the game at the lower level.

There is a great danger that Origin or the Super league Grand Final will be looked upon as the pinnacle in a player's career rather than pulling on a jersey to represent their country. Playing for their country should always be the ultimate ambition for any player. Look at American baseball, they have a 'World Series' but only American teams play. Origin is the same, only Australians play in that series and it only involves players from New South Wales and Queensland, so how can it be the top of the tree? At the time that I am writing this there is a World Cup competition, but here in Australia you would never know from the media. Yet we got six weeks of over exaggerated hype during the three origin games!

My own club here, Cronulla, do very little to support the junior side of the game in the area. In 1989 the Saints sent out a colts side to play down here. When they arrived to play the Sharks colts side, the game was not played at Shark Park but at a Rugby Union ground at Sylvania. The club would not let their own colts team play on the first team pitch. After the game the Saints players were invited back to the Cronulla ground for a meal but the Sharks colts players were not! That is not the way to develop the junior side of the game. The game up country here in Australia is dying from a lack of funding from the top. The authorities actually think that by sending two teams out into the country to play a league game is going to solve the problems that country football faces, it doesn't. If bush football dies then some stars of the future will never get the opportunity to actually play the game and come through to the top.

The influence of television in the game and the money it brings in is not something that is new. Don't for one minute think that television is interested in promoting the game; they are not. What they are interested in is promoting their company and products. Way back when I was at Saints we were due to play in a BBC 2 Floodlit Trophy game at Knowsley Road. I was captain at the time and when I got home after work there was a 'pea-souper' of a fog. I rang the club to see if the game had been called off only to be told no it had not and the club could not call it off. I tried to say that we could not see so how could we play. Basil Lowe said to me, 'We are contracted to play and the BBC control us so we play.' When I got to the ground, having struggled to drive down the East Lancs Road through the fog, I walked out to the end of the tunnel and, even with the extra floodlights the BBC had brought that they needed for the colour broadcast, I could not see the goal posts five yards away and still the club was not allowed to call off the game. It was only when the show's producer rang through to the club to say he was stuck in heavy fog in Bolton and could not get to the ground in time that the BBC called off the game. Even back then it was a case of the tail wagging the dog. Today it is a very big tail wagging on a very small dog with regard to Rugby League, particularly here in Australia.

I am told it is the same situation back in England, the lion's share of television money goes to the Super

League clubs and the rest of the clubs pick up the scraps. Super League clubs in England tend to place demands on the game that are designed to help them rather than the game as a whole. That is no way to develop the game and it is not going to lead England back to the top of international Rugby League. People running the Super League clubs need to look past the end of their noses and realise that international rugby is vital for the survival of the game. They just don't see it, or don't want to see it. As I said we are in a rut and until we get out of it, if we ever do, then Australia will always be the top of the tree.

When I played it was England, Australia and France with New Zealand nowhere on the international scene. Now it is New Zealand and Australia and the rest nowhere. When you look at the New Zealand side now, most of the players are playing in the NRL, not in their own domestic competition and that is why they are now so strong. If the South Sea Islanders like Fiji and Tonga continue to grow stronger by their players coming into the NRL, then England will move even further down the pecking order. Yet fundamentally the game has not changed, the idea is to score more points than the opposition, to get the ball and put it down over the opposition try line. When the opposition have the ball hit them low, hit them hard and hit them often. That is the game, when did it stop being a game and become a business?

Why are we following the Aussies in everything they do? We used to produce great creative Rugby League players and every club had them, players like Alex Murphy, Frank Myler, Vince Karalius, Frank Pitchford, Harold Poynton, Eric Ashton, Billy Boston, Neil Fox, Brian McTigue, I could go on and on. Now all we produce are clones of the Australian players. We seem to have little influence in the international arena and so have let the Aussies dictate just how the game should be run. The so called International Board is now a joke as the Aussies change rules but do not go to the board for their permission, they simply do as they please. We have seen two referees officiating at a match and they have even had four linesmen at games. Rules are altered to speed up the game and so on. We now have a bloody bunker where a bloke sits up on high and makes a decision on a game being played miles away. What people forget is we can have all the technology but in the end it comes back to a single man in a bunker making a human decision. In my playing days we called him the referee or sir. Sure he made mistakes but we simply got on with the game.

That Australian attitude is both arrogant and bad mannered but we in England seem powerless to challenge them. Come on England take the Aussies on off the bloody field, take back control of the game we gave to the world. The Aussies of course think they run the game and change the rules to suit themselves – and of course to suit the demands television companies place on their game. When will we catch up and beat the Aussies? Never until we get out of the rut we are in, stand tall and go back to playing the creative game we used to play.

Make the game more competitive once again by either getting rid of the interchange rule or reducing the number of changes a team can make during the game. That will ensure that players play for longer on the field and less on the bike on the sideline and so will get fatigued more. It is then that the creative players will come into their own. Rugby League has always prided itself on entertaining the people who come to watch. They really do not pay to watch five charges and a kick to the corner, and unless the game changes folks will stop watching. We have just had the play-off games here in Australia and the double header only attracted just over 30,000. Aussie Rules Football a week earlier in Sydney attracted 94,000, yet we still bury our head in the sand and think there is nothing wrong. At the start of the 2014 season here in Sydney, 27,000 turned up to watch the Sydney Roosters play the South Sydney Rabbitohs, on the same weekend over 40,000 turned up to watch Sydney FC play Western Sydney Wanderers in a soccer game.

We need to wake up before it is too late. It is time for the English authorities to take back the game they evolved and stopped pussyfooting around with the Australian and New Zealand authorities. They need to run the game and stop pandering to the Super League clubs, and if the clubs don't like it then they can go their own way and we will see just how long they last. Remember it is the game that is important not individual clubs. Whatever happened to the International Board? In my day countries could not mess around with the rules of the game, every change had to be approved by the International Board. Now as I said the folks in Sydney think they can make whatever changes they like and to hell with the International Board, and sadly they can.

Until the British start to exert some authority, the Aussies will continue to run the game as they see fit, or more accurately as the television companies see fit. Come on England get some balls and take the game back!

6

Off Field Honours

When I finally retired from the game I expected to have a quieter life, after all the game goes on and new players grace the field. Fans seem quickly to forget what former players did for their club as they watch the present day stars on the pitch. I did, and still do, get the odd request for an interview from the Aussie press and television but I felt my time was over. It just shows how wrong you can be.

When the Super League troubles came along in the mid-1990s, they had a greater effect in Australia than in England, but once it all settled down we had the ill-fated World Club Challenge back in 1996. The idea was simple enough; Australian clubs would play English clubs home and away, and eventually there would be a Grand Final. What a load of rubbish. The whole competition was ill thought out and badly managed, but having said that, I did get a trip back to St. Helens on the strength of it.

My old team Saints had been drawn in the same section as the Sharks, and when the Cronulla club was over in England, St. Helens arranged for Tommy Bishop and myself to fly over when the two clubs met. As we had both played for the two clubs, the St. Helens past players association felt it was a good idea. Tommy and I were introduced to the crowd before the game and we had a lovely time and we attended the past players dinner.

The British sides got wiped out and all the competition did was highlight the huge difference in fitness, ability, attitude and commitment between players from the two countries. It also set the game back internationally a decade or more!

Then in 2003 I was contacted by the Cronulla club and told that I had been selected, or elected, whichever is the correct terminology, as one of the club legends. I have to say that I was very proud to be honoured in such a way, after all it had been 30 years since I last pulled on a Cronulla shirt. In the time the club has been in existence they have had a good number of players to choose from, and I was only with the club for three seasons. I think that in those early days of the club's existence they did not have the money or the kudos to attract a big name Australian player. I along with Tommy Bishop were perhaps the 'big names' at the club, even though we had travelled over from England.

Never-the-less I was delighted to be so honoured by the Sharks, and was even more delighted when in 2006 the club officials announced that they were to select a 'dream team'. This would be players that had played for the club since its inception that it was felt were the greatest players to pull on a particular shirt for the Sharks. When the club contacted me and told me I had been selected as one of the props in the dream team I was very chuffed. The team they selected was:

Full back: David Peachey

Wing: Mat Rogers

Centre: Steve Rogers

Centre: Andrew Ettingshausan

Wing: Ray Corcoran

Stand-off: Chris Wellman

Scrum-half: Tommy Bishop

Prop: Jason Stevens

Hooker: Ron Turner

Prop: Cliff Watson

Second-row: Ken Maddison

Second-row: Gavin Miller

Loose forward: Greg Pierce

14: Dane Sorenson

15: Steve Kneen

16: Brett Kimmorley

17: Mark McGaw

In truth I suppose they did not have many top class props to choose from, not being in existence for that long. But none-the-less they selected me and I felt that the club had paid me a very great honour. To become a legend and member of the dream team was for me even sweeter because, although it was something I had achieved for my efforts on the field, the selection was made a long time after I had thrown my boots in the dustbin down in Helensburgh.

It was not until four years later that I was to get a phone call that would really blow my mind. It was in 2010 and, in truth, I had not been following the English game too closely by then, so I was not really up to speed on what was happening at St. Helens. When the phone rang and I picked it up I heard this Pommie accent on the other end of the line. The caller was Tony Colquitt, the Chief Executive of the club, and he asked if I was Cliff Watson. I told him that I was and he then informed me that the club was to leave Knowsley Road after 120-odd years. They were to share the Widnes ground for a season until the new stadium they had planned was completed. As part of the celebrations, the club had got together with members of the Rugby League media and the Past Players Association and selected what he called the greatest 17 St. Helens players, and that they had selected me as one of the props.

Tony could have knocked me down with the proverbial feather when he told me. He went on to say that the club would be flying me and my wife over to England and they would put us up in a top hotel for seven days. It was then that I got a bit worried, I thought this bugger is winding me up, having a joke at my expense. I took a bit of persuading that the guy was on the level and what he was actually telling me really was true. I was racking my brains to work out who could be behind the wind up as I believed it to be. To check he was on the level, I actually rang him back on the English number he gave me, and confirmed that the invitation was for both Barbara and myself. It was only then that it sank in just what an honour this was.

Saints had been playing professional Rugby League for 115 years and, in that time, I cannot imagine just how many great props had turned out for the club. I know from my time there that the likes of Alan Prescott, Abe Terry, Albert Halsall and Eric Chisnall had played prop. Prescott was my first coach at the club when I signed and a legend in the game, so for me it was the greatest honour I had ever received. I had won every honour the game had to offer on the pitch and I think I was the most capped player in the club's history, but to be selected as one of the greatest 17 players was just mind blowing. I was in pretty good company when I found out just who they were. The first 13 is: Paul Wellens, Tom van Vollenhoven, Doug Greenall, Paul Newlove, Alf Ellaby, Les Fairclough, Alex Murphy, Alan Prescott, Keiron Cunningham, Cliff Watson, Dick Huddart, Vince Karalius. The substitutes are: Sean Long, Chris Joynt, Paul Sculthorpe and Kel Coslett.

It was the most wonderful experience to return to the club once more to be part of the celebrations, and also to meet up with the likes of Tommy Voll, Kel Coslett, Alex Murphy and Dick Huddart, all of whom I had been privileged to play alongside. It was without doubt the greatest time I have ever had in the game and all of this came after I had left the club four decades earlier. It is an honour I treasure as high as any cap or medal I have ever won – if not higher.

My wife and I flew over to Manchester and the club put us up in a five star hotel. We had a great time, even though it was a little sad to see the end of the old stadium that held a lot of happy memories for me. As people say, time marches on, and the need for change is always there, so it was inevitable given the way the game was going in England that the club needed a new venue. Now it is all about corporate sponsorship and the likes. People want greater comfort, entertainment and such like before they will part with their brass, and a new stadium provided facilities for the 21st century. I was able to savour, for the last time, the fond memories I had of the ground and the players I had played with and against. I was also a little sad as I thought of those great players I had the privilege of playing with who were no longer with us – Vince Karalius for one and Bill Sayer another, and as I walked onto the field once more I am sure I heard Bob Dagnall shout to me, 'Pull him down Cliff'.

She was a good old girl was Knowsley Road and she did alright by me, so God bless her. I was very grateful for the privilege of having graced the place and the honour of being there to help celebrate the passing of the ground. I will admit that there was perhaps a little tear in my eye as I walked off the pitch for the last time.

*****

I do not think that in England the game pays the tribute that it should to former great players. I know that club support is tribal, and Saints fans would not say they liked or admired any player from another club. It is the same in Australia but not quite to the same extent. Here a player who has done it for club and country seems to gain the respect of everyone in the game and does not get quickly forgotten. John Raper and Reg Gasnier are idolised here in Australia, but Vince Karalius and Eric Ashton are all but forgotten back home and that is not right. The game in England needs to make better use of its former great players rather than simply letting them fade away once they stop playing or coaching. We will never be a national sport in England until former great players are recognised by all sportsmen and women in their own country.

Sportsmen and women from other sports seem to be idolised by the supporters. Bobby Charlton, Tom

Finney and Stanley Matthews are a case in point, as are Mary Peters and Kelly Homes in athletics, while Gareth Edwards and J.P.R. Williams are still revered in Rugby Union. With our game it seems to be a case of 'the king is dead, long live the king.' I know we have the Hall of Fame, but do the authorities really make the most of that? It seems they are more interested in promoting the 'Man of Steel' concept, which is no bad thing, but it is simply promoting present day, or more accurately, present season stars. Let's start displaying a great deal more pride in what past players have done for the game. Let's start honouring all of those players who have contributed to making our game so great.

7

The Best of the Best

Whenever I am chatting with fans, either here regarding the Cronulla Sharks or fans out from England about St. Helens, the conversation always seems to come round to who were the best players that I had the privilege of playing with during my career. In writing this book, I had for the first time to really address this question seriously. It struck me that the Australian part of the question is relatively easy, simply because I was only with the club for three seasons. However, I'll deal with St. Helens first as that is where I started the game and where I spent most of my playing career.

When I thought about who I would choose as the best players from St. Helens, I decided that I would select a team that I would have liked to take on the field with me when I was captain of the side. The second criteria I used was to select only players that I played many times with. It was then that the problems began because of two factors; firstly I spent 11 years at the club and so there were a great many players to choose from, and secondly Saints were a top side when I played and a great many international players pulled on a jersey alongside me. However, these were the players that made it into my 'Greatest St. Helens 17': Kel Coslett, Tom van Vollenhoven, Billy Benyon, Peter Harvey, Len Killeen, Tommy Bishop, Alex Murphy, Albert Halsall,

Bill Sayer, Cliff Watson, Ray French, John Mantle, Vince Karalius. Subs: Wilf Smith, Eric Chisnall, John Warlow, Les Jones.

There were a good many more I would like to have selected but I can only have 16 to play alongside and these made the team for the following reasons.

Full Back: Kel Coslett

I considered Austin Rhodes but I only played a short time with him, so even though he was a great full back, he did not make the criteria I had set. Also coming into contention was Frankie Barrow as he seemed to have some sort of magnetic quality that drew the opposition toward him so that he could tackle them. In the end I went with Kel. Kel came from Welsh Rugby Union and he had as safe a pair of hands as anyone I have seen in the game. Defensively he was very strong with a superb kicking game. He could kick out of hand well and was a very accurate goal kicker. He was not the fastest player but he did not need to be as the full back tended not to link into the three quarters as much back then. You just knew that it was going to take something special to get past him at the back.

Wing: Tom van Vollenhoven

You simply could not leave Tom out of any team. He was a finisher supreme when given a chance, and if you did not give him a chance he would simply make his own. He had a great step but was deceptively strong for his size. His defence was also outstanding and he would often cover across the field to tackle players attacking down the other wing. When he came to Saints he spoke very little English, being fluent in Afrikaans. He could take a knock and would get up looking for more. He was actually a policeman in Rhodesia before coming over and quickly became a crowd pleaser and favourite at the Saints. He would be in any team simply on the number of tries he scored in his career.

Centre: Peter Harvey

This choice may well surprise a lot of people but I've included Peter simply because he would do whatever was asked of him, and do it well. His defence was sound and he could read a game very well being equally at home playing at stand-off if he was needed. He was one of those 'unsung heroes' that all teams need and you knew he was never going to let you down, however big the game was. He had great consistency and I never saw him have a bad game.

Centre: Billy Benyon

Billy was not the biggest centre in the world but certainly one of the hardest tacklers. Very little ever got past him. He was also a good attacking player who had a little side step off either foot. He could read a game very well and in open field he rarely put a foot wrong in either attack or defence. His defensive qualities were such that it allowed his wingman Len Killeen to flourish. Len knew that Billy was never going to give him a hospital pass and so responded to that by playing with greater confidence with Billy inside him. He should have won more caps than he did but I think it was his size that held him back when the selectors were picking the teams. For Saints he was Mr. Reliable.

Wing: Len Killeen

Another South African that came over from Rugby Union. Len was not the strongest defender in the team, but when he played alongside Billy Benyon he did not need to be. Len was a finisher of the highest quality due mainly to his speed. He did not possess a side step of any description, but once given a gap to run at, very few could catch him. He could also kick goals for fun, and if Coslett was off with his kicking or out injured you knew Len would kick the extras for you. Len was a big game player, the bigger the game the better he would perform and nothing phased him. At Wembley against Wigan in 1966 he walked away with the Lance Todd Trophy after almost winning the game on his own. Like Tommy Voll you could not leave him out of your team.

Stand-Off: Alex Murphy

In my opinion Alex was the complete footballer. When I first played with him I could not believe the acceleration he possessed. He could pick a ball out of the scrum and be away before anyone even moved. A great football brain with speed of thought to match his pace. You could have it any way you wanted with Alex, he was not one to be put off by the roughhouse tactics in the game back then. When it came to playing football he was in a class of his own. A world class player whether at stand-off, scrum-half or centre, he was peerless.

Scrum-Half: Tommy Bishop

Tommy was the ultimate competitor, he wanted to win every game and win whatever the cost. He came to Saints from Blackpool Borough via Barrow where he had played for Lancashire in a game that had impressed the Saints board so they went out and signed him. He was always nagging you on the field and pushing the team forward. On one occasion in a cup game I recall he dropped a goal and he kept going on after the match about how his drop goal had won the game for us, he forgot about the other forty-odd points we scored that afternoon. That was Tommy, a competitor to the very end and a terrier like scrum-half of the old school.

Prop: Albert Halsall

Albert had begun his career as a wingman so still had a great deal of speed for a prop. He would follow Tommy Bishop around the field, waiting for the pass which would put him in the clear. He was a great defender and never shirked his tackling. He was also not one to turn away from a bit of a bust-up either. He and I had one when he was at Salford the week before he signed for Saints. Sadly Albert never came to terms with the four and six-tackle rule which destroyed his career as he refused to adapt to the new game, but he had the lot – good hands, speed, a bit of biff, and a good scrummager.

Hooker: Bill Sayer

Bill came to Saints after being shown the door by his home town club Wigan. He was never the quickest player about the park, but you could bet your mortgage on him winning the scrums in a match by at least two to one. In the unlimited tackle game that ability was priceless. At Saints he emulated the achievements of his Wigan career. He was a character as well but was as tough as teak and his ball winning skills won many a game for Saints. I would reckon he was the best hooker I ever played with, and that is why he is in the team rather than Bob Dagnall who was also a very good hooker and ran Bill very close.

Second-Row: Ray French

Ray was the workhorse that every team needs if they are to be successful. I considered Dick Huddart but felt I did not play enough games alongside him to put him in the team. Ray was all arms and legs, and many times I would be making a tackle when Ray would come in as second man and almost flatten me along with the opposition. When he left Saints for Widnes he had developed into a bit of a ball distributer as well, but he would primarily be in my team simply because of the phenomenal stamina and work rate he possessed.

Second-Row: John Mantle

John came from Welsh Rugby Union and was a big, strong, quick and powerful runner who could also tackle and was not averse to a bit of knuckle if that was called for. He was also a quick learner. When Karalius left for Widnes and we played them, John said to me that Vince was an old man now and past it and he was going to spend the game running all over him. He tried it once and said to me, 'Cliff, I think it would be better if I ran round him in future'. Like I said, John was a quick learner. He developed into a world class second-row in the end and would be in anyone's team.

Loose Forward: Vince Karalius

Vince was a legend in the game, but when I joined Saints I wondered why he had been nicknamed 'The wild bull of the Pampas' by the Aussies. After playing with him for a while I found out. He was as tough as they come and took no prisoners in the tackle. He wanted the ball all the time and I sometimes felt we needed two balls on the field – one for Vince and one for the rest of us. He was also a great ball distributor and would often flick a pass out just before his elbows hit the ground and so catch the opposition out. Murphy always knew it was coming and would be there to take the pass. I know that he was not over keen on the Aussies and he frightened the crap out of Rex Mossop when he toured Australia. He was a superb all-round player and fully deserved his reputation.

Sub: Wilf Smith

Wilf was another workhorse who was our three-quarter equivalent of Ray French and rarely, if ever, had a bad game. It was for that reason he tended to be taken for granted as it was always expected that Wilf would be in the team and would do the job. For me though he had one precious quality that was often unseen off the field, and that was the ability to keep Alex Murphy in check. Alex could sometimes be a bit hot-headed and start his own private battle with the opposition. Wilf would see this before anyone else and he would chide and chivvy Alex to get back on track. He won many a game for Saints simply by keeping Alex's head right.

Sub: Eric Chisnall

Eric was a local lad who came into the team and into his own as a replacement for Ray French. He didn't quite have Frenchy's work rate but he was an excellent ball distributor and was a good second-row or prop. He was also fast, could avoid a tackle and had a good offload. Eric became a good all-round player who notched up over 500 appearances for Saints, he was strong in defence and could be relied on to produce the goods for the side.

Sub: John Warlow

John was another player who came to Saints from Welsh Rugby Union. He was what I call a bog or mud-runner. Unlike Eric Chisnall who ran on top of the ground, John ran well through the mud of the English Winter. He and I sat on the bench at New Zealand's Carlaw Park in the 1968 World Cup campaign when the coach picked 'Fancy Dans' to play on a quagmire of a pitch when what was needed was mud runners like John. He was a fierce tackler who hurt players when he tackled them. John was another who was not averse to using a bit of knuckle if the situation demanded it.

Sub: Les Jones

Les was a very good wingman who, when he first broke into the side, would come in off his wing to crash tackle the centre in much the same way that Mick Sullivan used to do. He got in trouble with the disciplinary and so later on he seemed to stop doing it as much. I suppose being sent off does that to you! He was a good finisher who always ran bravely for the line, and if there was half a chance then Les would usually score. I gave him the nod over the likes of people like Frank Wilson, another Welsh lad who was a very good wing or centre during my time at the club. However, I felt that Les had the edge and so he got the last spot on the bench.

*****

It was only after I had selected my preferred players that I realised just how great a team Saints were when I actually played for them. Of the 16 players plus myself, five of them: Kel Coslett, Tom van Vollenhoven, Alex Murphy, Vince Karalius, and Dick Huddart, actually gained selection for the Saint's Greatest 17. I myself was honoured to be in that greatest group as well, so there are six of us in that squad. That is quite remarkable I think and goes some way to explaining why we were so successful over that decade I played for the club.

When I was asked to consider the best players to have with me from my time in Cronulla, the choice was much simpler. The reasons for that are firstly I only played at the club for three seasons, and secondly they had few international players at the time. I therefore decided that I would select what I considered to be the best Cronulla team that I played in, and when I did that the choice was simple. I went for the players that took to the Sydney Cricket Ground for that 1973 Grand Final against Manly. That was, as a team, the best I ever took to the field with. They were: Warren Fisher, Ray Corcoran, Steve Rogers, Eric Archer, Bob Wear, Chris Wellman, Tommy Bishop, Ron Turner, Graham Bowen, Ken Maddison, John McGuire, Greg Pierce and Rick Bourke.

Full Back: Warren Fisher

Warren was a good full back and whilst not the biggest of players nothing frightened him. He always wore his heart on his sleeve. He had come from bush football and was as hard as nails. He had a great defence and linked up well in attack.

Wing: Ray Corcoran

Ray was the best wingman while at the same time probably the worst wingman. He would beat three or four players then, faced with an open run to the try line, would go back and try to beat them all over again. He had a great side step and on his day was brilliant. He did not have the strongest defence but his flair in attack made up for that.

Centre: Steve Rogers

Steve played in the Grand Final whilst still only a teenager. He had great pace but early on in his career tended to drop off tackles. However, he worked on that and as his career developed his defence got much better. He was also a great goal kicker but was unfortunate to miss a couple in the Final. He developed into a good player and represented Australia more than 20 times.

Centre: Eric Archer

Eric was a great player who, funnily enough, started his career as a prop forward! He rendered down and ended up in the centre for us. He was very strong on defence and he always protected his wingman. He would never pass to his wingman if there was nothing on but would take the tackle. When his wingman did get the ball he always had room in which to work.

Wing: Bob Wear

Bob joined Cronulla from Barrow and was at the club when I arrived. He was another blessed with pace and he scored a lot of great tries. He had this knack of timing his crash tackle on a centre so that he took man and ball. He also had an eye for the interception. He was a good reader of the game, even from out on the wing.

Stand-Off: Chris Wellman

There was only one Chris Wellman, he was as hard as they come and never stopped trying during a game. He would always give 110 per cent and would happily run through a brick wall for the team. He was not the biggest but was a great utility as he could play stand-off, centre and even second-row.

Scrum-Half: Tommy Bishop

Tommy was the same in Australia as he had been in England. As a player/coach he led by example and never asked a player to do something he would not do himself. He had no fear and had that cheekiness to try whatever he liked on the field, and usually it came off.

Prop: Graham Bowen

He was for me the complete front row forward. He was a great scrummager, had pace and a bit of a side step to go with it. Graham was good in defence and took the ball up well. He never shirked when the hard yards had to be made and was a good reader of the game. As I said the complete prop.

Hooker: Ronnie Turner

Ronnie was an Australian international when I joined Cronulla, and I had played against him in the 1970 World Cup back in England. He came from bush rugby and was really quite tall for a hooker. You could rely on him to win his own ball, and more often than not he would hook the ball against the head for you. He was quick about the field and also had fast hands. A great ball winner.

Second-Row: Ken Maddison

A great competitor, Ken had been a centre at St. George and had moved to the second-row at Cronulla. He was an 80 minute player who was good in both attack and defence. He went on to tour England in 1974 with that great Aussie touring team.

Second-Row: John McGuire

He was probably the most underrated player in the side. John could use a ball and would put players through a gap with a little short pass. He was the workhorse of the team in the Ray French style and he helped me to settle in when I arrived at the club.

Loose Forward: Greg Pierce

Greg was a great lock and had good speed. He and Ken Maddison could be relied on to break the line every time they went on the field. Greg used to create gaps that players then took advantage of. A great reader of the game and of his team-mates, he went on to captain his country.

Sub: Rick Bourke

Rick was a youngster in the side and, in my opinion, had great potential. He was a rangy wing or full back who had a great ability to see a gap and get into position to go through it if he got the ball. His defence was always strong and he rarely missed a tackle. He was just 20 in that Grand Final.

*****

Once again if you look at that team, seven of them were named in the 2006 Cronulla Dream Team, so we must have been a decent side. I feel that the team did not get the breaks or the luck it deserved. It was a well-balanced team from one to 13 and, had it been allowed to stay together, who knows what it would have achieved. I have written earlier, as have others, about the team being allowed to disintegrate which was a pity as I felt we could have dominated the competition for the next few years after that 1973 Grand Final.

8

Thanks

As a young kid running around just after the war ended, I suppose like many boys I wanted to be a fireman or train driver or footballer when I grew up. They were the usual occupations kids dreamt of becoming on leaving school. What never entered my head was becoming a professional Rugby League player.

When I left school I felt my life was mapped out, as it was for many working class folk back then. I had a job as an apprentice tool-maker and felt that I would have a job for life once I qualified. My then girlfriend Barbara and I were saving up to buy a house and get married. We would have children and I was content to play social Rugby Union and pay for the privilege. Thankfully my life was turned upside down by one simple advertisement placed in the *Sporting Chronicle* by Basil Lowe, the then Secretary of the St. Helens club. Equally important that newspaper was read by the guy I worked with for a time in the stores who saw the advert and mentioned it to me.

To say that the game of professional Rugby League changed my life would be the biggest understatement of all time. I played the game at the very highest level on two continents. It took me from the West Midlands up to the North West of England and finally over to Cronulla in Australia. It was a roller coaster journey of 17 years and I would like to thank all of those people, players and coaches that helped to make it possible for me to achieve what I did in the game.

First and foremost my thanks must go to my wife, Barbara, who has been with me and supported me every minute of this journey that began back in 1960. She and our daughters: Gaynor, Tina, and Kareena, have had to make sacrifices in order that I could do many of the things I did on the field. Barbara, while enjoying watching tennis, was never keen on Rugby League. I think it was the cold weather that put her off because she watched more games in the warm climate in Sydney than she ever did in St. Helens.

Secondly, to my old boss at Newey Brothers back in Dudley, I would like to say thanks for putting me in the stores when I broke my wrist. Had he not done so I would never have seen the advert in the *Sporting Chronicle*.

It would be remiss of me not to thank Harry Cook, Basil Lowe and the rest of the Saints board who in 1960 showed great faith in me and signed me for the club. And to all of the coaches that I was lucky enough to play under. I learned something from each of them. A special thanks to the great Alan Prescott who took a raw Rugby Union prop and helped turn me into an international player through his belief and perseverance.

To all of those players, far too many to mention by name, that I was lucky enough to actually play with and form a friendship with go my sincere and heartfelt thanks. To all those fans who watched me play – whether they liked or hated me – I respected them as their hard-earned cash helped pay my wages at the end of the week.

Last but by no means least, a great big thank you to

the sport of Rugby League. Truly it really did change my life. I owe the game so much, long may it thrive and long may it keep taking youngsters just like I was and forever changing their lives for the better. Perhaps that is why it really is 'the greatest game'.

Cliff Watson
Playing Record

Rugby Union

Dudley Kingswinford

First game Saturday September 24th, 1955 for the newly formed Colts team, 15 years and six months old at the time.

In all games for the club: 112 appearances, nine tries, 27 points.

Three appearances for Hereford and Worcester Combined Counties.

Total number of Rugby Union games played: 115.

Rugby League

St. Helens

Signed for St. Helens in August 1960.

367 appearances, 6 substitute appearances, 57 tries, 171 points.

Cronulla Sutherland

Moved to Australia in 1971.

39 appearances, nine tries, 27 points.

Wollongong Wolves

Signed for Wollongong Wolves in 1974 and played two seasons as player/coach.

34 appearances.

Illawarra District

Three appearances.

International Teams

Great Britain debut in second Test against Australia in 1963.

30 Test matches played plus 27 tour and other games. Also three games for England.

Total Number of First Grade Appearances in Rugby League

St. Helens	373
Cronulla	39
Wollongong Wolves	34

International matches	60
Illawarra District	3
Total	509

Honours

St. Helens

Five Lancashire Cup wins.

Three Lancashire league wins.

Two Challenge Cup wins.

Two Championship wins.

One Player's No 6 win.

Three Mackeson Period wins.

Two Mackeson Merit Table.

International

Two Great Britain tours (1966 and 1971).

Two World Cups (1968 and 1970).

Test series from 1963 to 1971

Captained England against Wales in 1968.

Cronulla

Thiess Cup 1971.

Grand Final runner up 1973.

Wollongong Wolves

Minor Premiership winner and Grand Final runner up 1974.

Off Field

Elected one of 17 greats with St. Helens 2010.

Elected one of the Cronulla Legends 2003.

Elected to Cronulla Dream Team 2006.

In total Watson played: 115 Rugby Union games.

                                    509 Rugby League games.

                                    624 first grade games.

Last but by no means least, Watson is the only player to be awarded THE ANDY CAPP.

About the Authors

Cliff Watson is a very modest man who felt, when approached about his autobiography, that there were other ex-players whose stories were better suited to be the subject of a book. Once he began relaying his tale it was obvious that he was a natural storyteller.

Cliff still lives in Miranda not too far away from the Cronulla Sharks ground. He goes about his retirement in the same, old unassuming manner but is still involved in the game he loves. He is an active member of the 'Men of League' organisation and travels around New South Wales raising money for players or their families who have fallen upon hard times. When not doing that he is happy pottering in his garden and attending to his aviary of zebra finches and canaries.

Tom Mather now lives in retirement in the Illawarra with his wife, Janet, after leaving teaching in England. He has written many books covering the history of the game of Rugby League, the latest being Cliff Watson's autobiography.

Tom is a great believer in recording the history of the game as it was before the Super League era. Recently he completed an ebook project to cover all of the Rugby League tours down under between the two World Wars, feeling the players of the past deserved to have their exploits brought back into the public domain. In doing so, this allows present day supporters to see just how much is owed to those stars who played before television imposed its influence on the game.